12-16-15
GB
$27.49

Medical Assisting
Test Prep
Study Guide for the
CMA and RMA

Authored by: David Merlino

How To Use This Study Guide

This study guide was designed to be used by students preparing for the CMA exam, or for students who want to brush up on content while still in school. This study guide encourages active participation of the student, allowing the student to learn as if they were in a school setting. This study guide was designed to give students the most important information, the information most likely to be seen on the exams, without the filler information. This gives the student the most effective and efficient way to study.

To utilize this study guide and gain the most benefit from it, the student will:

- Fill out the fill-in-the-blank study guide, as much from memory as possible, then with the aid of the full study guide.
- Complete all assignments given, including matching, crossword puzzles, etc.
- Take the practice exams, making sure to utilize test-taking techniques discussed momentarily.
- While taking practice exams, student should answer questions on a separate piece of paper, which will give the student multiple attempts at taking the test without the answers being written in the book.

If adhered to, the previous steps will fully prepare the student to pass the licensing/certification examination.

Table of Contents

Study Skills

- Do not do all of your studying the night before or day of the test. Study consistently, up to several times per week. Cramming is good for short-term learning, but does not help with long-term learning. The more you study, the more likely you are to retain the information.
- Use all of your class and home work as study materials. The information in these assignments is information that might be on your exam.
- Take many short breaks as you study. Memory retention is higher at the beginning and end of study sessions than it is in the middle. Study for no longer than ten minutes, then take a short break.
- Focus on one subject at a time while studying. You don't want to confuse yourself by mixing information.
- Study the subject you have the most difficulty with more than subjects you are comfortable with. Studying what you aren't weak in doesn't help. If you need work on a specific subject, focus the majority of your time learning that information. Not studying this information could prevent you from passing the exam.
- While studying, take notes on important information, especially if it's information you don't recognize or remember. Use this information to study with.
- Assign yourself tests, reports, assignments and projects to complete. You are more likely to remember information if you write a report on it than if you just read the information.
- Teach information you are studying to another person. If you are responsible for someone learning something, you have to know and understand the material, and be able to put that information into the simplest terms possible, so someone else can understand it. This will only help you.
- Understand the material you are studying. Do not just try to memorize certain answers you think may be on the test. Certain "key words" might not be on the test. Learn everything about a subject, and you'll never get any question on that subject wrong.

Test-Taking Tips

- Go to the restroom before taking the exam. Using the restroom beforehand ensures that you are 100% focused on the exam, and not on your bladder.
- Do the easiest problems first. This will help boost confidence, give you information you can use on other questions, and ensure that you have enough time to finish the exam.
- Read the entire question slowly and carefully. Never make assumptions about what a question is asking. Assuming you know what a question is asking may lead to you missing key words in the question that tell you exactly what the question is asking. Read every single word in every single question, multiple times if necessary. Understand what the question is asking before you try answering it.
- Identify key words in each question. Key words are words that tell you exactly what the question is asking. Identify these words easily by reading questions aloud to yourself. The words you find yourself emphasizing while reading aloud are likely the key words.
- If you don't know an answer, skip it and return to that question later. The information in the question may be found later on in the test, and may help you answer the question. Always be on the lookout for information you've previously seen in the test. If you find information you've seen, make sure to go back and look at the previous question to see if anything helps you answer the question.
- Do not change your answers, unless you misread the question, or found information at another point in the test that helps you answer that question. Changing your answers puts doubt into your mind, and leads to more changing of answers. The answer you put first is usually correct. Do not change your answers!
- Match key words in the answers with key words in the questions. Sometimes it's as simple as matching terms, if you've exhausted all other avenues.
- Eliminate answers you know aren't correct and justify the reason they aren't correct. If you can eliminate one answer from each question, that

brings your odds of getting that question right up to 33%. If you can eliminate two answers that can't be right, that brings it up to 50%. Then it's just a coin flip!

- Read the entire question before looking at the answers. Again, never make assumptions about what the question is asking.

- Come up with the answer in your head before looking at the answers. If the same answer you come up with is in the list of answers, that's most likely the right answer.

- Read every answer given to make sure you are picking the most correct answer. Some questions have multiple right answers, and you need to make sure you're picking the most correct answer.

- Make sure you are properly hydrated before the test. Studies have been done on the affects of proper hydration on those taking tests. People who are properly hydrated tend to score higher than those who are not.

- Exercise for twenty minutes before the exam. Exercise has also been shown to increase test scores.

Reducing Test Anxiety

- Study consistently. If you understand the material, you won't be as stressed out about the test. There are ways you can study without this book or your class notes as well. An example, whenever you take a bite of food, think about every structure the food passes through in the alimentary canal and what each of the organs do.
- Keep a positive attitude while preparing for the test and during the test. If you think you're going to fail, you will not be as motivated to study, you won't adhere to your test taking techniques, you'll become stressed out during the exam much more easily, and you'll be more likely to fail.
- Try to stay relaxed. Utilize deep breathing techniques to calm down if you start feeling nervous or stressed. You will have over two hours to finish the exam. You can afford one or two minutes to calm yourself down if you need to.
- Exercise consistently up until the test to reduce anxiety. Exercise has been shown to significantly reduce stress, and also helps with memory retention. Try utilizing flash cards while riding an exercise bike.
- Answer the easy questions first to help boost confidence. You'll start to see that the exam isn't that difficult, and you'll feel much more positive about it.
- Take your time on the test. If you find yourself rushing, slow down. Do not rush through it. You may miss important information in the exam and answer questions incorrectly because of this.

Medical Terminology

Medical terminology is widely used throughout the medical field, and is the primary way of communicating with other health-care professionals. Medical terminology has origins in Latin and Greek. A medical term consists of three parts: The word root, which is what the term is mainly talking about; the prefix, which comes at the beginning of the medical term; the suffix, which comes at the end of the word. Both the prefix and suffix help to further describe what may be happening in a certain medical condition.

Word Roots

Abdomin/o: _____
Acr/o: _____
Aden/o: _____
Adip/o: _____
Angi/o: _____
Ankyl/o: _____, _____
Arteri/o: _____
Arthr/o: _____
Ather/o: _____ _____
Audi/o: _____
Aur/o: _____
Bi/o: _____
Brachi/o: _____

Bucc/o: _____
Carcin/o: _____
Cardi/o: _____
Cephal/o: _____
Chlor/o: _____
Chol/e: _____
Cholecyst/o: _____
Chondr/o: _____
Cirrh/o: _____
Col/o: _____ _____
Corp/o: _____
Cost/o: _____
Cry/o: _____

Cutane/o: _____

Cyan/o: _____

Cyst/o: _____

Dent/o: _____

Derm/o: _____

Dist/o: _____

Dors/o: _____

Embol/o: _____

Emphys/o: _____

Encephal/o: _____

Enter/o: _____ _____

Erythr/o: _____

Esophag/o: _____

Gastr/o: _____

Gingiv/o: _____

Gloss/o: _____

Gluc/o: _____

Hem/o: _____

Hepat/o: _____

Hist/o: _____

Home/o: _____

Hydr/o: _____

Hyster/o: _____

Inguin/o: _____

Jaund/o: _____

Kerat/o: _____

Kinesi/o: _____

Kyph/o: _____

Lact/o: _____

Later/o: _____

Leuk/o: _____

Lip/o: _____

Lord/o: _____

Mamm/o: _____

Mast/o: _____

Melan/o: _____

My/o: _____

Myel/o: _____

Nas/o: _____

Necr/o: _____

Nephr/o: _____

Neur/o: _____

Ocul/o: _____

Onc/o: _____

Oophor/o: _____

Oste/o: _____

Path/o: _____

Ped/o: _____

Phleb/o: _____

Phren/o: _____

Pneum/o: _____

Proxim/o: _____

Pulm/o: _____

Pyr/o: _____

Ren/o: _____

Rhin/o: _____

Salping/o: _____ _____

Scler/o: _____

Scoli/o: _____

Somat/o: _____

Spondyl/o: _____

Stomat/o: _____

Thorac/o: _____

Ventr/o: _____

Prefixes

a-: _____

ab-: _____

ad-: _____

af-: _____

an-: _____

ana-: _____

ante-: _____

anti-: _____

auto-: _____

bi-: _____

brady-: _____

circum-: _____

contra-: _____

di-: _____

dia-: _____

dys-: _____, _____

ef-: _____

endo-: _____

epi-: _____

exo-: _____

homeo-: _____

hyper-: _____

hypo-: _____

infra-: _____

inter-: _____

intra-: _____

iso-: _____

macro-: _____

mal-: _____

meta-: _____

micro-: _____

mono-: _____

multi-: _____

neo-: _____

pan-: _____

para-: _____

peri-: _____

poly-: _____

post-: _____

pre-: _____

pseudo-: _____

quadri-: _____

retro-: _____

supra-: _____

syn-: _____

tachy-: _____

tri-: _____

uni-: _____

Suffixes

-ac: _____

-al: _____

-algia: _____

-ar: _____

-blast: _____

-cision: _____

-clast: _____

-crine: _____

-cyte: _____

-derma: _____

-ectomy: _____

-edema: _____

-emia: _____ _____

-esis: _____

-ferent: _____

-gen: _____

-globin: _____

-ic: _____

-ician: _____

-icle: _____

-ist: _____

-itis: _____

-lysis: _____

-oid: _____

-osis: _____

-pathy: _____

-phagia: _____

-phasia: _____

-physis: _____

-plasia: _____

-plegia: _____

-pnea: _____

-poiesis: _____

-rrhage: _____ _____

-rrhea: _____

-stasis: _____

-tomy: _____

-trophy: _____

-uria: _____

Anatomy and Physiology

Anatomy: The study of the _____ of the human body.

Systemic Anatomy: The study of the body's _____ _____.

Regional Anatomy: The study of the different _____ of the body.

Physiology: The study of the _____ of the human body.

Cells: Cells are the functional units of all tissues, and they perform all essential life functions.

Cellular Mitosis: A cell _____ from one mother cell into two daughter cells in order to replace cell loss.

Organelles are found _____ cells to make the cells function.

Nucleus: Contains _____, controls activity inside cells.

Nucleolus: Forms _____ and _____ _____ in ribosomes.

Mitochondria: Produce _____.

Golgi Apparatus: Allows _____ _____ _____ in cells.

Smooth Endoplasmic Reticulum: Synthesizes _____ and _____.

Lysosome: _____ _____ _____ inside cells.

Ribosome: Contain _____ _____ _____, assemble cell proteins.

Cytoplasm: _____ _____ _____ inside cell.

Homeostasis: Homeostasis is the existence and maintenance of a _____ _____ _____. Several factors contribute to the homeostatic process, including hormones, nerve impulses, and sweating.

Homeostatic Mechanisms: Homeostatic mechanisms are _____ things that happen in the body that alter the internal environment in response to a specific change. _____ reduces body temperature, and _____ increases body temperature.

REGIONAL ANATOMY

There are three main regions of the body:

Central
Upper Limb
Lower Limb

Central Body Region: The Central body region contains everything in
the center of the body, such as the _____, _____, and _____. The trunk can
be further divided into three other regions:
Thorax: The thorax(thoracic) contains our major internal organs, such as the
_____ ___ _____. Also inside the thorax is the _____, a form of
connective tissue that surrounds organs inside the chest(except the lungs),
protecting them from too much jostling.
Abdomen: The abdomen contains the majority of our digestive organs,
including the stomach, liver, gallbladder, pancreas, small intestine, large
intestine, kidneys, and spleen.
Pelvis: The pelvis contains our _____ _____ _____, the
_____ _____ _____ _____, and the _____ _____.

Body Cavities: Body cavities _____ ___ ____ ____. There are two
main body cavities:
Dorsal Body Cavity: Made by the _____ ___ _____ _____,
contains the _____ ___ _____ _____.
Ventral Body Cavity: Made by the three trunk cavities(_____, _____,
_____).

Directional Terms: Used to describe structures in the body in relation
to other structures or body parts.
Superior: Above
Inferior: Below
Anterior: Front
Posterior: Back
Proximal: Closer to the midline

Distal: Further from the midline
Medial: Middle
Lateral: Side
Deep: More internal
Superficial: Towards the surface

Body Planes: There are _____ _____ _____ used to divide the body.
Sagittal: Splits the body into _____ _____ _____.
Midsagittal: Splits the body into equal ____ and ____ ____, runs down the _____ of the body.
Transverse/Horizontal: Splits the body into _____ ____ _____.
Frontal/Coronal: Splits the body into _____ ____ _____.

TISSUE

There are _____ types of tissue in the human body:
Epithelial, Nervous, Muscular, and Connective.

Epithelial: Forms most _____, the _____ _____, and the _____.
Epithelial tissue is responsible for _____ the body, _____ nutrients, and _____ substances. Epithelial tissue is _____ and contains no blood vessels.

Nervous: Forms the _____, _____, and _____ that emerge from both. Nervous tissue allows for _____, _____ _____, and _____ of skeletal muscle.
A _____ is a _____. It contains a _____, the site of cell function. It also contains _____, branch-like projections that come off the cell body to receive nervous impulses, bringing them into the cell body.

Muscular: There are three types of muscle: _____, _____, _____.
Skeletal: Connects to the _____ and allows _____ _____.
Cardiac: Muscle of the _____, responsible for _____ _____ throughout the body.

Smooth: Found in locations such as the _____(arrector pili) and _____ _____. Responsible for actions such as _____.

Connective: Connective tissue is formed by the "_____ _____",
materials you don't find in cells. They can contain _____, _____ _____, and _____. Connective tissue is responsible for actions such as _____ structures, _____ structures, _____ of nutrients, _____ and _____ the body, and _____ the body.
Blast Cells: Immature cells that _____ the matrix.
Clast Cells: _____ _____ the matrix.
There are several types of connective tissue, including _____, _____, _____, _____, _____, _____, _____ _____, and _____. The most abundant form of connective tissue in the body is _____.

Blood: Consists of _____, _____, _____, and _____.
Erythrocytes: Also called ___ _____ _____, responsible for _____ oxygen and carbon dioxide throughout the body via _____, which is found in the cytoplasm of the cells.
Leukocytes: Also called _____ _____ _____, they are _____ that help fight off infectious agents and break down dead cells and debris inside the body.
Thrombocytes: Also called _____, they are responsible for _____ the blood.
Plasma: The _____portion of blood, allows _____ of blood cells throughout the body.

Serous Membranes: Forms of connective tissues that _____ organs inside body cavities, preventing the organs from creating friction. There are ___ serous membranes inside the _____: the _____, which surrounds the _____ and the _____, which surrounds the _____. There is ___ serous membrane that is found inside the _____and _____ that separates the organs from the muscle on top of them: the _____.
Inner wall of a serous membrane: _____ serous membrane
Outer wall of a serous membrane: _____ serous membrane

12

BODY SYSTEMS

Cardiovascular System: Responsible for _____ _____ throughout the body, bringing oxygen, hormones, and nutrients to tissues, and eliminating carbon dioxide and waste products from the body. Consists of the _____, _____ _____, and _____.

Heart: Pumps blood throughout the body. Consists of the superior vena cava, inferior vena cava, right atrium, tricuspid valve, right ventricle, pulmonary valve, pulmonary arteries, pulmonary veins, left atrium, bicuspid valve, left ventricle, aortic valve, and aorta.

Blood Vessels: Create _____ for blood to travel throughout the body.

Arteries: Largest and most internal blood vessels, move blood _____ _____ _____ _____, and almost always carry oxygenated blood.

Veins: Move blood _____ _____ _____, and almost always carry deoxygenated blood.

Capillaries: Microscopic blood vessels used to transport oxygen-rich blood _____ _____.

Pathologies of the Cardiovascular System:

Anemia: Decrease in _____ _____ ability of the blood, most commonly due to a lack of _____, _____, or both. Causes fatigue due to _____.

Aneurysm: _____ of a wall of an artery outward, caused by a _____ arterial wall. Most likely the result of _____ putting strain on the arterial wall. May break open, resulting in severe _____ internally, which may be fatal.

Angina Pectoris: _____ in the _____ resulting from myocardial ischemia. Pain may also radiate into the _____ _____.

Arteriosclerosis: _____ of the walls of arteries, caused by a lack of elasticity in the arteries. Reduces circulation, which may lead to _____.

Atherosclerosis: Buildup of _____ _____, or _____, on the walls of the arteries, reducing blood flow. May result in _____ and the formation of _____ _____.

Embolism: A _____ _____ or _____ _____ freely moving throughout the circulatory system. May become lodged in the heart, lungs, or brain, resulting in lack of blood flow to those structures, causing _____.

Endocarditis: Inflammation of the _____ _____ of the heart as a result of infection.

Heart Murmur: Flow of blood _____ in the heart due to malfunctioning _____, typically the bicuspid or mitral valve. Formation of _____ _____ may occur, along with fatigue.

Hypertension: _____ _____ _____, 140/90 mm Hg. Results in inelasticity of the arterial walls, reducing circulation.

Migraine: _____ headache. Caused by _____ of extracranial blood vessels, which puts substantial pressure upon the _____, producing intense pain. May be caused by stress or smoke, among other things.

Myocardial Infarction: Death of _____ _____, usually caused by a blockage in the _____ _____, which are responsible for supplying the myocardium with blood.

Pericarditis: Inflammation of the _____, usually the result of an infectious disease.

Phlebitis: Inflammation of a ____, caused by trauma, pregnancy, prolonged periods of sitting or standing, and may present with _____ _____.

Raynaud's Syndrome: Constriction of _____ _____ in the ____ ___ _____, which reduces blood supply. Caused by cigarette smoking, cold exposure, or stress.

Transient Ischemic Attack: Temporary _____ dysfunction resulting from _____ in part of the brain. Also known as a " _____ ", it can be a precursor to a more serious stroke in the future.

Varicose Veins: Swollen veins, caused by dysfunction in the _____ inside the veins, resulting in blood pooling down the legs and forcing the veins towards the surface of the body.

Digestive System: Responsible for bringing food _____ ____ _____,
_____, _____ of nutrients, and _____ of waste.
Oral Cavity: Also called the _____, contains the _____, _____ _____, and _____. Performs _____ and _____.
Pharynx: Also called the _____, allows _____ of food from the oral cavity to the esophagus.
Esophagus: Tubular organ that allows _____ of food from the pharynx to the stomach.
Stomach: _____ and _____ _____ food into usable, absorbable nutrients.
Liver: Filters harmful chemicals from the blood, produces _____.
Gallbladder: _____ _____ and _____ _____ into the duodenum.
Pancreas: Produces _____ and _____ and secretes these substances into the duodenum.
Small Intestine: _____ nutrients into the body for use. Consists of the _____, _____, and _____.
Large Intestine: _____ _____, converts chyme to _____, assists in _____ of waste.
Between organs in the Digestive System, we have _____. Sphincters are _____ _____ bands of _____ that allow food to pass through into other organs, and to _____ food from going _____ in the digestive tract.
There are four main sphincters in the digestive tract:
Esophageal Sphincter: Located between the _____ and _____.
Cardiac Sphincter: Located between the _____ and _____.
Pyloric Sphincter: Located between the _____ and _____ _____.
Ileocecal Sphincter: Located between the _____ _____ and _____ _____.

Pathologies of the Digestive System:

Cholecystitis: Inflammation of the _____, usually due to a blockage of the _____ _____, stopping the flow of ___ into the duodenum. Blockages most commonly caused by _____.

Cirrhosis: Destruction of _____ cells, resulting in the formation of adhesions and fibrous material in the _____, causing the _____ to become a yellowish-orange color. _____ function is gradually impaired.

Crohn's Disease: _____ disorder which affects the _____ tract, resulting in _____ and _____ of the mucous membranes, in which scar tissue can develop.

Diverticulosis: Development of small _____ that protrude from the walls of the _____ _____, caused by weakening of the walls due to a lack of substances for the walls to press against.

Diverticulitis: Inflammation of _____ _____, which may become abscessed and develop ulcers.

Gastroenteritis: Inflammation of the _____ **of the** _____ and _____ _____, most commonly caused by food poisoning or emotional stress.

Gastroesophageal Reflux Disease: Hydrochloric acid flowing from the _____ upwards into the _____, producing a burning sensation. May result in ulcers in the esophagus.

Hepatitis: Inflammation of the _____ most commonly associated with a _____ _____, which may be acute or chronic. Results in pain, nausea, fatigue, diarrhea, and jaundice in the acute stage of infection.

Hernia: _____ of an organ through the surrounding connective tissue membrane. May result in pain and impaired body function, depending on the location and herniated structures involved.

Ulcerative Colitis: Autoimmune disorder resulting in _____ of the _____ of the _____ _____, producing ulcerations. May result in bloody stools, diarrhea, and weight loss.

Endocrine System: Responsible for _____ the specific activities

of cells and tissues via _____ release. Endocrine glands secrete hormones directly into the _____ _____.

Pineal Gland: Secretes _____. The exact role of the pineal gland is unknown.

Pituitary Gland: Secretes _____ _____, _____, and _____-_____ hormones. Responsible for _____ in bones, production of _____, and production of _____ cells in women and _____ cells in men.

Thyroid: Secretes _____ and _____, responsible for increasing _____ production.

Parathyroids: Secrete _____ hormone, which raises concentration of **calcium** in the blood.

Adrenals: Secrete _____ and _____, which elevate _____ _____, increase _____ _____, and increase _____ _____.

Pancreatic Islets: Secrete _____ and _____. Insulin _____ glucose concentration in the blood, while glucagon _____ glucose concentration in the blood.

Ovaries: Secrete _____ and _____.

Testes: Secrete _____.

Pathologies of the Endocrine System:

Addison's Disease: Autoimmune disorder which results in the _____ of the _____ _____, causing a decrease in adrenal function.

Cushing's Disease: Over-production of _____, resulting in increased weight and muscle atrophy.

Diabetes Mellitus: Increased levels of _____ in the blood stream. Diabetes Type I is caused by a _____ in _____ _____ in the body, which restricts the breaking down of glucose, while Diabetes Type II is caused by the body being _____ to _____, which is then unable to break down glucose.

Goiter: Enlargement of the _____ _____, commonly seen with hyperthyroidism, hypothyroidism, inflammation, or a lack of _____ in the diet.

Grave's Disease: Autoimmune disease resulting in _____, anxiety, trembling, and fatigue. May also result in protrusion of the eyeballs.

Hyperthyroidism: Increased _____ function, results in a _____, hypersensitivity to heat, increased appetite, and increased respiration.

Hypothyroidism: Lack of _____ hormone in the body, results in fatigue, weight gain, edema, and sensitivity to cold.

Integumentary System: Contains the ____, ____, ____, _____ _____, ___ _____, and _____ _____. Responsible for _____, _____ of substances, _____ of substances, and detecting _____.

Skin: Made of epithelial tissue, skin is avascular and is used for _____.

Sudoriferous Glands: Secrete _____, which is a homeostatic mechanism. Sudoriferous glands are forms of exocrine glands.

Sebaceous Glands: Secrete _____. Sebaceous glands are forms of exocrine glands.

Sensory Receptors: Detect _____ in the skin.

Pacinian Corpuscles: Detect _____ pressure.

Meissner's Corpuscles: Detect _____ pressure.

Thermoreceptors: Detect differentiations in _____.

Nociceptors: Detect _____.

Pathologies of the Integumentary System:

Acne: _____ infection of the skin, due to numerous factors, including _____ production, stress, and hormonal imbalance.

Athlete's Foot: Also called _____ _____, it is a highly contagious _____ infection found on the feet, primarily between the toes, which may result in breaking of the skin and lead to bacterial infection.

Basal Cell Carcinoma: _____ serious, _____ growing, _____ common form of skin cancer, usually due to overexposure to sunlight.

Burns: First degree burn – Most common, least serious. Most common form is a sunburn, affecting the _____, resulting in inflammation and irritation of the skin.

 Second degree burn – Burn moves _____ the _____ into the _____, which leads to the development of _____ and swelling.

 Third degree burn – Burn moves _____ the _____ and the _____, into the _____ _____. Results in _____ and scarring of the skin, and may lead to infection if not treated properly.

Cellulitis: Acute infection caused by _____ or _____ bacteria, which often enters the body through exposure to _____, affecting nearby tissues. Presents with well-defined borders of inflammation.

Decubitus Ulcer: Also known as a _____ _____ or ____ ___, results in _____ caused by prolonged _____ placed on a part of the body, causing _____ and ultimately _____ of the affected tissue.

Eczema: Idiopathic disorder causing _____, ___, ____ ____ of skin. May be either acute or chronic.

Herpes Simplex: Highly contagious chronic _____ infection, resulting in _____ _____ around the mucous membranes.

Hives: Also known as _____, it is an inflammatory reaction in response to exposure to an _____ or _____ _____. May be either acute or chronic, depending on the cause.

Impetigo: Acute _____ infection caused by staphylococci or streptococci, results in sores that form around the mouth, nose, and hands. Mostly seen in _____, it is highly contagious.

Lice: Highly contagious _____ infection, found in hair. Produce egg sacs called "nits".

Malignant Melanoma: Over-production of _____, resulting in formation of tumors that may spread to other regions of the body. A = Asymmetrical, B = Border, C = Color, D = Diameter, E = Elevated.

Mole: Benign skin lesion, resulting from an increased amount of _____ in an area.

Psoriasis: Autoimmune disorder in which the body's immune system attacks _____ tissue. Epithelial cells quickly regenerate at a rate quicker than normal, which results in _____, ___, _____ patches of skin.

Ringworm: Also known as _____ _____, it is a _____ infection resulting in circular raised patches on the skin.

Rosacea: A form of _____, results in a _____ _____ that appears across the nose and cheeks. Exacerbated by exposure to cold.

Scleroderma: An autoimmune disorder, resulting in excessive _____ production in the skin, causing the skin to become _____. Can be a sign of organ failure.

Sebaceous Cyst: Blockage of a _____ _____, resulting in the body forming a thick membrane of connective tissue around the gland, limiting tissue damage as a result of infection.

Squamous Cell Carcinoma: Form of skin cancer which develops into an area of _____, caused by overexposure to sunlight, or may be found in the mouth of a person who chews tobacco or smokes cigarettes.

Wart: Epidermal protrusion resulting from infection by the _____ _____ _____. Results in increased _____ production on the area of infection.

<u>Lymphatic System</u>: Consists of _____ _____, _____ _____, _____, and _____ _____.

Lymph Vessels: They are a ___-____ system, meaning lymph in the vessels only flows one direction. The vessels _____ foreign bodies and nutrients from tissue.

Lymph Nodes: A lymph node is a _____ of lymph tissue, responsible for _____ and _____ foreign objects, helps to _____ _____.

Lymph: Made of mostly water, protein, leukocytes, urea, salts, and glucose.

Spleen: Removes old _____ _____ _____ from the blood stream.

Thymus: Produces __-_____(T-cells).

Pathologies of the Lymphatic System:

Acquired Immunodeficiency Syndrome: Immune disorder caused by ___, which destroys the body's __-____, effectively disabling the immune system.

Allergies: _____ of the body to agents which are normally harmless in most people.

Chronic Fatigue Syndrome: _____ disease which results in symptoms such as _____, _____-_____ _____, and _____.

Lymphedema: Increased amounts of _____ _____ in a limb, resulting in _____. Caused by inflammation, trauma, or blocked lymph channels.

Lupus: _____ disorder affecting the _____ _____ of the body, resulting in a rash across the face, scales on the skin, fatigue, fever, photo-sensitivity, and weight loss.

Mononucleosis: _____ infection, resulting in a high fever, fatigue, sore throat, and swollen lymph nodes.

Pitting Edema: Swollen area, leaves ___ in the skin after applying pressure. May be a sign of _____ _____.

<u>**Muscular System**</u>: Contains _____. Muscles are responsible for _____ and _____ _____.

In order for a muscle to contract, _____ must be present. The contractile unit of a muscle is called a _____. Sarcomeres are formed by _____ filaments(_____) and _____ filaments(_____).

Muscle Contractions: A contraction is when _____ in a muscle _____.

Isometric Contraction: The _____ of a muscle _____ _____ _____, but _____ in the muscle _____.

Isotonic Contraction: The _____ in a muscle _____ _____ _____, but the _____ of the muscle _____.

Concentric Contraction: The _____ in a muscle _____, and muscle _____ _____.

Eccentric Contraction: The _____ in the muscle _____ _____ _____, and muscle _____ _____.

Prime Mover/Agonist: The muscle of a synergist group _____ _____ _____.

Synergist: A muscle that _____ the prime mover in performing the action.

Antagonist: A muscle that _____ the prime mover, performing the _____ action.

Fixator: A muscle that _____ an area so an action can be performed.

Pathologies of the Muscular System:

Adhesive Capsulitis: Formation of _____ that stick the _____ _____ to the head of the _____, severely restricting the range of motion at the shoulder joint. May also be caused by hypertonicity of the subscapularis.

Atrophy: Loss of _____ _____ due to lack of use or malnourishment.

Drop Foot: Paralysis or severe weakness of the _____ _____, placing the ankle into forced _____. May also be caused by hypertonicity of the gastrocnemius.

Fibromyalgia: Inflammatory disease affecting muscles and connective tissue, resulting in _____, numbness, tingling sensations in the limbs, and fatigue.

Golfer's Elbow: A form of _____, results in inflammation and pain located at the _____ _____ of the _____. The _____ of the wrist are affected, as they originate on the medial epicondyle of the humerus.

Muscular Dystrophy: _____ disorder, resulting in _____ of muscles. Muscle degeneration leads to _____ and lack of use, eventually resulting in paralysis and deformity.

Strain: An injury to a _____ or _____, may be caused by overexertion or overstretching.

Temporomandibular Joint Dysfunction: Pain in the _____ upon opening and closing, _____ at the temporomandibular joint, and decreased range of motion. Results from trauma to the joint or muscles, clenching of the teeth, grinding of the teeth, stress, or a combination of the previous causes.

Tendonitis: Inflammation of a _____, results from injury to either the tenoperiosteal or musculotendinous junction.

Tennis Elbow: A common form of _____, results in inflammation and pain located at the _____ _____ of the _____. The _____ of the wrist are affected, as they originate at the lateral epicondyle of the humerus.

Torticollis: Spasm of the _____ unilaterally, forcing the head to lean to _____ _____. _____ may result.

Whiplash: Straining or spraining of tendons, muscles, and ligaments in the _____ due to violent _____ motion of the head and neck. As a result, tendons, muscles and ligaments may be injured and weakened, with an increase in headaches, pain, and dizziness. Most commonly seen in _____ _____.

Nervous System: There are two branches of the Nervous System, the **Central Nervous System** and **Peripheral Nervous System**. It also contains the **Autonomic Nervous System.**
Central Nervous System: Consists of the _____ and _____ _____.

Brain: Consists of the _____, _____, and _____ _____.
Cerebrum: The _____ part of the brain, split into left and right _____, responsible for _____ actions and _____ reception. Each hemisphere contains _____, named after bones overlaying them.
Frontal Lobe: Responsible for _____ motor function, _____, _____, _____.

Parietal Lobe: Responsible for processing most _____ information.
Temporal Lobe: Responsible for _____ and _____ processing, and _____.

Occipital Lobe: Responsible for _____ input.

Cerebellum: Responsible for _____ _____, _____, and _____.
Brain Stem: Contains three parts: _____ _____, _____, and _____.

Medulla Oblongata: Regulates the body's _____ _____.
Pons: Creates a pathway for _____ between the _____ and _____.

Midbrain: _____ _____.
Peripheral Nervous System: Contains _____. There are _____ pairs of _____ _____ that emerge from the spinal cord, and __ pairs of _____ _____ that emerge from the brain.
Cranial Nerves: Emerge from the brain, numbered via Roman numerals. Olfactory(I), Optic(II), Oculomotor(III), Trochlear(IV), Trigeminal(V), Abducent(VI), Facial(VII), Vestibulocochlear(VIII), Hypoglossal(IX), Vagus(X), Spinal Accessory(XI), Glossopharyngeal(XII)

Autonomic Nervous System: Responsible for maintenance of _____ within the body. There are two autonomic nervous responses in the body.
Sympathetic Response: Also called " _____-or-_____ ", when activated, increases _____ in the body, _____ heart rate. It also _____ _____ digestive organs and pulls blood from them for use in the muscles.
Parasympathetic Response: Also called " _____-and-_____ ", when activated, **decreases** heart rate, brings blood into the digestive organs to stimulate **peristalsis**. Controlled by Cranial Nerve X, the **Vagus Nerve**.

Pathologies of the Nervous System:

Alzheimer's Disease: Progressive _____ of _____ _____, resulting in loss of memory, dementia, confusion and disorientation.

Bell's Palsy: _____ of _____ of the _____ as a result of inflammation or compression of the facial nerve. May be permanent, or may subside.

Carpal Tunnel Syndrome: Compression of the _____ _____ by the transverse carpal ligament, resulting in loss of function and sensation in the hand.

Cerebral Palsy: Loss of muscle control and coordination due to _____ to certain parts of the _____ during early life stages such as infancy.

Encephalitis: _____ of the _____, most commonly caused by a _____ infection. The virus usually enters the body after contact with _____. Inflammation may result in necrotic brain tissue and death.

Hemiplegia: Paralysis of _____ _____ of the body, usually as the result of a **stroke**, which may impair function to specific regions of the body.

Meningitis: Inflammation of the _____. _____ meningitis is the most severe form, which may result in death. Symptoms include nausea, vomiting, dizziness, and headache. Highly contagious.

Multiple Sclerosis: Autoimmune disorder in which the immune system attacks the _____ _____ surrounding axons in the central nervous system, causing degeneration of the myelin. Degeneration also results in scarring on the axons, which results in severe pain in acute stages.

Paraplegia: Paralysis of the _____ _____ due to an injury to the spinal cord anywhere below the T1 segment. Loss of function results in muscle atrophy.

Parkinson's Disease: _____ or _____ due to reduced levels of the neurotransmitter _____ in the body. Affects fine motor movements at first, then affects larger movements as the disease advances.

Quadriplegia: Paralysis of the _____ and _____, resulting from an injury to the spinal cord between C5 and T1.

Sciatica: Compression of the _____ _____ by hypertonic muscles, most commonly the _____. Results in pain radiating down the leg, and may even reach the bottoms of the feet.

Trigeminal Neuralgia: Compression of the _____ _____, resulting in _____ _____ around the mouth, nose, and eyes.

Reproductive System: The reproductive system is divided into two

subcategories, _____ **Reproductive System** and _____
Reproductive System.
Male Reproductive System: Produces _____ and _____ _____.
Consists of the _____, _____, _____, and _____ that carry sperm.
Penis: Responsible for _____ _____, allowing passage of sperm and urine out of the body.
Testes: Found inside the scrotum, responsible for _____ of _____ and _____. Attach to the urethra via the _____ _____.
Female Reproductive System: Produce _____ _____, _____, and development of a _____. Consists of the _____, _____, _____ _____, and _____.
Vagina: Located between the cervix and the opening to the outside of the body. Allows a _____ for the penis during _____.
Ovaries: Glands that produce _____, or egg cells, and _____.
Fallopian Tubes: Allow _____ of an oocyte from the ovaries to   the uterus. _____ most often occurs in the fallopian tubes.

Respiratory System: Exchanges _____ and _____ _____

in blood, and aids in _____ _____ from the body.
Nose: _____ and _____ _____ coming in and exiting the body.
_____ air via _____.
Larynx: Tube at front of pharynx, strengthened by muscles. Contains the _____, which prevents food from entering the larynx during swallowing.

Allows _____.

Trachea: _____ inferior to the larynx, allows _____ of ___ into lungs.

Bronchi: Split into right and left, divides into smaller branches as they move through the lungs. Smallest branches are called _____. They secrete _____ to trap dirt and debris, which is then expelled from the lungs by _____.

Alveoli: _____ _____ at the end of bronchial tubes, connect to blood vessels. Responsible for _____ of oxygen and carbon dioxide.

Diaphragm: _____ attached to base of rib cage and vertebrae, creates a vacuum to bring air _____ the lungs and expel air _____ the lungs. When the diaphragm _____, air _____ the lungs. When the diaphragm _____, air _____ the lungs.

Pathologies of the Respiratory System:

Apnea: _____ of _____, temporarily. Most commonly occurs during _____, commonly caused by compression of airways by the tongue or pharynx.

Asthma: Spasm of _____ _____ in the bronchial tubes, which is a reaction to stimuli such as _____ or _____ _____. Mucous production is also increased, further reducing air intake, creating wheezing sounds upon inhalation.

Bronchitis: Inflammation of _____ _____, with additional mucous production. _____ bronchitis is the side effect of a _____ _____ such as influenza, while _____ bronchitis is the result of irritants entering the lungs over a long period of time, such as _____ _____.

Cystic Fibrosis: _____ disorder producing _____ _____ throughout the respiratory tract, reducing air intake. Mucous blocks the _____ _____, limiting absorption of nutrients.

Emphysema: _____ of lung _____ due to exposure to irritants such as _____ _____, reducing oxygen intake and carbon dioxide output.

Influenza: Acute _____ infection, resulting in an inflamed pharynx and nasal cavity, increased mucous production, and fever.

Laryngitis: Inflammation of the _____ resulting in ____ of _____. Most commonly caused by an infection, but can be caused by cigarette smoke.

Pleurisy: Inflammation of _____ _____ surrounding lungs, resulting in a _____ _____ upon inhalation.

Pneumonia: _____ infection in the lungs, which fills the lung alveoli with fluid and waste products, reducing air intake.

Skeletal System: Contains _____. Responsible for _____ the body, _____ _____ _____, providing _____, and giving muscles a _____ to _____ to which permits _____.

Axial Skeleton: Consists of the ____, _____ _____, and _____ ____.

Skull: Protects the brain. Contains the following bones: Frontal, occipital, parietal, temporal, mandible, maxilla, sphenoid, vomer, nasal, ethmoid, lacrimal, and zygomatic.

There are four main sutures of the cranium, holding the bones of the skull together. They are:

Sagittal Suture: Connects the two _____ _____.

Coronal Suture: Connects the _____ _____ to the _____ _____.

Squamous Suture: Connects the _____ ____ and _____ _____.

Lambdoid Suture: Connects the _____ ____ and the _____ ____.

Vertebral Column: _____ the spinal cord. Contains ___ individual bones. _____ _____ vertebrae, _____ _____ vertebrae, _____ _____ vertebrae, ____ _____ vertebrae, ____ _____ vertebrae.

Thoracic Cage: Also called the _____ ____, _____ the organs inside the thorax. There are _____ _____ of ribs. The _____ _____ pairs are called ____ ____. The _____ ____ pairs are called ____ ____. ___ _____ are called _____ _____, and they do not attach to the sternum.

Appendicular Skeleton: Consists of the bones of the _____ and _____ _____, and the _____ and _____ _____.

Upper Limb: Contains the humerus, radius, ulna, carpals, metacarpals, and phalanges.

Carpals: Scaphoid, Lunate, Triquetrum, Pisiform, Trapezium, Trapezoid, Capitate, Hamate.

Lower Limb: Contains the femur, tibia, fibula, tarsals, metatarsals, and phalanges.

Tarsals: Calcaneus, Cuboid, Cuneiform I, Cuneiform II, Cuneiform III, Talus, Navicular.

Pectoral Girdle: Contains the clavicles and scapulae.

Pelvic Girdle: Contains the ilium, ischium, pubis, and sacrum.

Pathologies of the Skeletal System:

Ankylosing Spondylitis: Progressive _____ disorder resulting in _____ of _____ _____. Disc degeneration leads to loss of curvature of the spine, fusion of vertebrae together, and loss of motion at the site of bone fusion.

Baker's Cyst: Formation of a sac _____ the _____ as a result of _____ _____ leaking from the joint cavity.

Bursitis: Inflammation of a _____ _____, usually due to trauma to a bursa. Often presents with _____ _____, restricting range of motion at the site if around a joint.

Dislocation: _____ of a bone from its normal location, damaging tissues around the area. Severely weakens the joint following the dislocation, allowing for further dislocation to occur.

Fracture: A _____ in a bone. A _____ fracture remains _____ the skin, while a _____ fracture _____ _____ the skin.

Gout: Excessive _____ _____ buildup in the body, resulting in a severely inflamed _____ _____, and may also be seen in the arms and hands as well. Caused by an inability of the body to eliminate uric acid normally.

Herniated Disc: _____ of the gelatinous center of an intervertebral disc, known as the _____ _____, through the tough cartilaginous portion of an intervertebral disc, known as the _____ _____. Results in compression of spinal nerves, producing pain.

Kyphosis: Hyper-curvature of the _____ _____, producing a hump-back appearance. Also known as _____ _____. Can be caused by tight chest muscles, weakened back muscles, or other conditions such as osteoporosis or ankylosing spondylitis.

Lordosis: _____-_____ of the _____ _____, forcing the vertebrae anteriorly. Also known as _____. Can be caused by hypertonicity of the psoas major, or weakness in the rectus abdominis. May also result in overstretching of the hamstrings.

Osteoarthritis: _____ of the _____ _____ between articulating bones. Results in increased friction between the bones, causing pain and inflammation. Also known as "wear and tear" arthritis.

Osteomyelitis: Bacterial infection affecting the bone, which may enter into the _____ and _____.

Osteoporosis: _____ of bone tissue, due to a lack of _____ entering into the bones. Usually seen in _____-_____ _____, due to a lack of _____ production. Bones become thin and brittle, making them prone to injuries such as fracture.

Rheumatoid Arthritis: Autoimmune disorder in which the body's immune system attacks _____ _____ surrounding joints. Upon degeneration, the membrane is replaced by _____ _____, which restricts range of motion in the joints. Usually takes place at the metacarpophalangeal joints of the hands. The fingers are turned to a medial position, making function difficult.

Scoliosis: _____ curvature of the vertebrae, most commonly in the thoracic vertebrae. Can be caused by severely hypertonic muscles, congenital deformities of the vertebral column, and poor posture.

Shin Splints: Pain along the _____ _____ _____ of the _____, usually due to tearing of muscular attachments. Results from over-training, running or jumping on hard surfaces, wearing the wrong equipment, etc. Also known as medial tibia stress syndrome and periostitis.

Sprain: Injury to a _____, caused by overstretching or tearing of a ligament.

    Grade 1: Stretching of a ligament _____ _____.

    Grade 2: _____ _____ of a ligament that presents with _____ and inflammation.

    Grade 3: _____ _____ of a ligament which requires surgery to repair.

Urinary System: Consists of the _____, _____, _____ _____, and _____. Responsible for _____ of waste from the body, _____ of nutrients, and _____ _____.

Kidneys: _____ and _____ substances back into the body. Regulates the amount of _____ in the body. Inside each kidney, there are _____ _____ _____, which are responsible for reabsorbing vitamins, electrolytes, and water back into the blood stream.

Ureters: _____ urine from the kidneys to the bladder.

Urinary Bladder: _____ urine.

Urethra: **Transports** urine from the urinary bladder out of the body.

Pathologies of the Urinary System:

Cystitis: _____ _____ of the _____ _____, resulting in bloody urine, pain, and increased urination frequency.

Pyelonephritis: _____ _____ of the _____, usually results after obtaining cystitis.

Uremia: Excessive amounts of _____ in the _____ _____, usually a sign of _____ _____, caused by inability of the kidneys to filter properly.

Urinary Tract Infection: _____ _____ typically affecting both the _____ and _____ _____.

Vital Signs

Vital Signs: Indication of the body's ability to _____ _____. Temperature, pulse, blood pressure, and respiration are the primary vital signs.

Temperature may be measured in several different areas, utilizing a thermometer.

Oral/Sublingual: Thermometer inserted _____ the _____. Baseline temperature is 98.6 degrees Fahrenheit

Axillary: Thermometer inserted into the _____. Baseline temperature is one degree less than oral/sublingual.

Rectal: Thermometer inserted into the _____. Baseline temperature is one degree higher than oral/sublingual.

Aural: Measures temperature of the tympanic membrane _____ the _____.

Pulse: Used to determine _____ _____ and _____ _____.

Heart Rhythm: Regularity of _____ _____.

Heart Rate: Beats _____ _____.

Radial Pulse: Read at the _____ _____ of the wrist, most common site to read pulse.

Ulnar Pulse: Read at the _____ _____ of the wrist.

Apical Pulse: Read using a stethoscope at the _____ of the _____.

Brachial Pulse: Read at the _____ _____ of _____, commonly used to determine pulse of infants.

Carotid Pulse: Read at the _____, used to determine pulse in adults.

Femoral Pulse: Read at the _____ _____ _____, used to determine pulse in adults.

Popliteal Pulse: Read at the _____ of the _____.

Dorsalis Pedis Pulse: Read on the _____ _____ of the foot.

Blood Pressure: Pressure felt in arteries during _____ _____.

Systolic Pressure: Pressure felt in arteries as blood _____ _____ _____(heart beating).

Diastolic Pressure: Pressure felt in arteries when the heart is _____ (not beating).

In a blood pressure reading of 120/80, 120 represents the _____ _____, and 80 represents _____ _____.

Respiration: The act of _____. Measured by observing breathing pattern, rate, and depth of breath.

Inspiration: _____ of air to bring _____ into the body.

Expiration: _____ of air to eliminate _____ _____ and other waste.

Normal Vital Sign Ranges:

Temperature:
>   Infant: 96-100
>   1-5 years: 98-100
>   6-10 years: 97-99.5
>   11-15 years: 97.5-100.5
>   Adult: 97.5-100.5

Pulse:
>   Infant: 80-160 beats per minute
>   1-5 years: 75-130 beats per minute
>   6-10 years: 70-115 beats per minute
>   11-15 years: 55-110 beats per minute
>   Adult: 60-100 beats per minute

Blood Pressure:
>   Infant: 60-95/50-65
>   1-5 years: 80-100/50-70
>   6-10 years: 80-120/50-80
>   11-15 years: 95-135/58-88
>   Adult: 90-120/60-80

Respiration:
>   Infant: 25-40 breaths per minute
>   1-5 years: 20-30 breaths per minute
>   6-10 years: 18-25 breaths per minute
>   11-15 years: 16-25 breaths per minute
>   Adult: 12-20 breaths per minute

CPR and First Aid

CPR: Cardiopulmonary Resuscitation

First Aid:
Emergency Triage: Classifying injuries by _____, _____ _____, and _____ _____.
Universal Precautions: Treating every person and fluid as _____ or _____. Used to properly contain blood-borne pathogens. Wear _____ and other protective equipment, avoiding contact with blood.
Documentation: Taking note of patient _____.
Good Samaritan Law: Law designed to _____ person performing first aid or offering care to unresponsive persons _____ a medical setting.

Heat Injuries:
Heat Exhaustion: _____ body temperature with _____ _____.
Heat Cramps: _____ and involuntary spasming of muscles due to _____ and loss of _____.
Heat Stroke: _____ body temperature with _____ of sweating, due to extreme dehydration.

Cold Injuries:
Hypothermia: Body temperature dropping _____ ___ degrees Fahrenheit.
Frostbite: Formation of _____ _____ in soft tissues, resulting in _____ of affected areas.

Burns:
First degree burn: Most common, least serious. Most common form is a sunburn, affecting the _____, resulting in inflammation and irritation of the skin. Apply cold dressings and cold water to the affected area.
Second degree burn: Burn moves through the _____ into the _____, which leads to the development of _____ and swelling. Contact EMS, cover burned areas with sterile bandages.
Third degree burn: Burn moves through the _____ and the _____, into

the _____ _____. May also involve muscles, tendons, ligaments, and bones. Results in _____ and scarring of the skin, and may lead to infection if not treated properly. Contact EMS, cover burned areas with sterile bandages.

Rule of 9's: Used to determine extent of _____ by total body area involved.
    Head and Neck: 9%
    Right Arm: 9%
    Left Arm: 9%
    Right Leg: 18%
    Left Leg: 18%
    Thorax: 18%
    Abdomen: 9%
    Lower Back: 9%
    Groin: 1%
Chemical Burns: Rinse with water, contact EMS.
Thermal Burns: Rinse with water, contact EMS.
Electrical Burns: Contact EMS.

Wounds:
Open Wound: _____ of _____ or membrane which results in exposure of the underlying tissues.
Incision: A clean _____.
Laceration: A cut producing _____ _____.
Abrasion: _____ skin. Cleanse with soap and water, apply sterile bandage.
Puncture: _____ resulting from _____ _____. Allow to bleed for a few minutes, cleanse with soap and water, apply sterile bandage.

Bites and Stings:
Animal Bites: If bite results in _____, try to force bleeding to clear out bacteria. Cleanse with soap and water, apply sterile dressing.
Rabies: _____ infection transferred via saliva.
Insect Sting: Scrape skin with a hard, flat, sharp object such as a knife to remove _____. Cleanse skin with soap and water. If asphyxiation is suspected, contact EMS.
Snake Bite: Notify EMS, immobilize area _____ _____, cleanse

area with soap and water.

Spider Bite: Cleanse bite with soap and water, immobilize area _____
_____. Suggest patient seek medical attention.

Scorpion Stings: Cleanse bite with soap and water, immobilize area
_____ _____. Suggest patient seek medical attention.

Orthopedic Injuries:

RICE: Rest, Ice, Compression, Elevation.

Sprain: Injury to a _____, caused by overstretching or tearing of a
ligament. Recommend patient utilize RICE in acute stage.

    Grade 1: _____ of a ligament without tearing.

    Grade 2: _____ _____ of a ligament that presents with
bruising and inflammation.

    Grade 3: _____ _____ of a ligament which requires surgery to
repair.

Strain: An injury to a _____ or _____, may be caused by overexertion
or overstretching. Recommend patient utilize RICE in acute stage.

Fracture: A _____ in a bone. A _____ fracture remains _____
the _____, while a _____ fracture breaks _____ the _____.
Immobilize area using splint.

Poisoning:

Inhalation: Introduced to the body via _____. Examples include carbon
monoxide or carbon dioxide. Patients might be given antidote, and require
breathing support via oxygen mask.

Injection: Introducing harmful substance into the body via _____
_____, _____, _____ _____, or _____. Usually
requires use of antidote to combat poison.

Absorption: Introduced into the body via skin _____. Examples include
_____. Area should be cleaned thoroughly with water.

Ingestion: Introducing harmful substances via _____. Depending on
substance, patient may require induced vomiting or drinking milk or water.

Instruments

Percussion Hammer: Used to test _____, may also be known as a
_____ _____.

Tuning Fork: Tests _____.

Nasal Speculum: Instrument inserted into the _____ that open the nasal passages, allowing for further visual inspection.

Otoscope: Allows visual inspection of the _____ _____ inside the ear.

Audioscope: Used to test the loss of _____.

Ophthalmoscope: Examine the _____ _____ of the _____.

Stethoscope: Used to listen to various _____ throughout the body, such as _____ _____, _____ _____ and _____ _____.

Laryngoscope: Used to examine the _____.

Vaginal Speculum: Instrument inserted into the _____ ____ that opens the vagina. Used primarily during ____ _____ and examination of the pelvis.

Anoscope: Used to examine the _____ and _____ _____.

Proctoscope: Used to examine the _____ and _____ _____.

Sigmoidscope: Used to examine the last portion of the _____ _____.

Autoclave: Used to _____ instruments. _____ chamber increases _____, _____ chamber _____. Uses steam above ____ _____ _____.

Forceps: Used to _____, _____, or _____ tissue or equipment.

Scissors: Used to _____ bandages, _____, and _____.

Scalpel: Small _____ used to perform _____ or _____ tissue from the body.

Retractor: Holds layers of tissue _____ to allow tissues underneath to be accessed.

Sutures: Used to _____ _____.

Skin Staples: Type of _____ used that must be removed when the would has _____ completely.

Dressings: Used on _____ to prevent further introduction of microorganisms. Secured to the body using _____.

Nebulizer: Delivers medication in _____ form via inhalation.

Electrocardiograph: Also called _____ or _____, measures the cycle of _____ _____ passing through the heart.

12-Lead Electrocardiograph: Uses _____ _____ to record _____ _____ information. Consists of _____ _____, _____ _____ _____, and _____ _____.

Single-Channel Electrocardiograph: Uses ___ ___ to record information.

Microscope: Used to view objects _____ _____ to the naked eye.

Catheter: Tube inserted into the _____ _____.

Centrifuge: Device used to separate _____ from _____.

Hemocytometer: Microscope used to count _____ _____, _____, etc. Most common type is _____.

Urinometer: Measures the specific _____ of _____.

Refractometer: Measures _____ of _____ through a _____.

Spirometer: Measures _____ of air intake and output.

Sphygmomanometer: Measures _____ _____.

EKG/ECG:

P Wave: Represents _____ of the _____ _____ and _____ _____, visualization of firing of the _____ _____.

PR Interval: Time it takes for a _____ _____ to travel from the ____ _____ through the _____ into the _____.

QRS Complex: Represents the _____ of an electrical impulse from the _____ of _____ through the _____.

ST Segment: Represents _____ of the _____ _____ and _____ _____.

T Wave: Represents _____ of the _____ _____ and _____ _____.

Artifacts: _____ in an EKG reading caused by ___-_____ _____.

Intentional Artifacts: May be caused by _____.

Medications and Injections

Local Anesthetics: Used to _____ an area which _____ _____.
Commonly _____ is used. Administered via _____ _____.
Analgesics: _____ relievers.
Antacids: Reduces activity of _____ in the stomach.
Antibiotics: Combats _____ growth, specifically _____.
Anticoagulants: Reduces formation of _____ _____.
Antifungals: Destroy _____.
Antihistamines: Reduces effects of _____ on the body.
Anti-inflammatory Agents: Reduce _____.
Antipyretics: Reduce _____ _____.
Antivirals: Combat _____ reproduction.
Broncho-dilators: Dilate _____ _____.
Decongestants: Reduce _____ in _____ _____.
Diuretics: Increases _____ production by _____.
Insulin: Helps control _____.
Sedatives: _____ and _____ the body.

Ampule: Small _____ container, broken at the neck to access medication.
Vial: Glass or plastic container sealed by a _____ _____ at the top.
Needles: Used to administer _____.
Gauge: _____ of a needle. The _____ the number gauge, the
_____ the needle diameter. The _____ the number gauge, the
_____ the needle diameter.

Types of Injections:
Intradermal: Injection into the _____ at a __ degree to __ degree angle.
Subcutaneous: Injection into the _____ _____ of the skin at a ____
degree angle.
Intramuscular: Injection _____ the _____ at a ____ degree angle.

Common Injection Sites:

Intradermal: Anterior _____, posterior ____, _____, _____ region.

Intramuscular: _____, _____ _____, _____, _____.

Subcutaneous: Posterior and lateral _____, abdomen around the _____, anterior _____.

Nutrition

Seven Nutrients: Proteins, carbohydrates, fats, minerals, vitamins, fiber, water.

ADA recommends 65% _____, 25% _____, 15% _____.

Vitamin A: Most common type is _____ - _____, found in orange and yellow fruits and vegetables. Maintains healthy _____, _____ membranes, _____, and _____.

Vitamin K: Blood _____.

Vitamin D: Produced in the _____ when exposed to the sun, also fortified in many foods. Allows the body to absorb _____.

Vitamin E: Found in vegetable oils, nuts, leafy vegetables. Helps to protect tissue from _____ _____, assists in the formation of _____.

Vitamin C: Found in citrus fruits and melons, assists in the body's _____ and protection of tissue from _____ _____.

Vitamin B6: Assists in the production of _____ and _____. Deficiency can result in _____.

Vitamin B12: Assists in formation of _____. Deficiency can result in _____ _____.

Potassium: Helps with _____ _____ and synthesizing _____.

Calcium: Most _____ mineral in the body. Provides _____ _____, allows _____ _____.

Iron: _____ for oxygen and carbon dioxide transport.

Sodium: Maintains _____ balance, helps transport _____ _____.

Magnesium: Maintains _____ _____, regulates _____.

Letterhead: Business stationary. Lists name, address, phone, usually at top of paper. 8.5" x 11" is standard. 8.5" x 14" is legal.

Envelopes: A number _____ envelope is known as "business size", measures 4 1/8" x 9 1/2". Invoices and statements use envelopes sized between number 6, measuring 3 5/8" x 6 1/2", and number 10. Contains transparent windows to show address.

Pre-addressed Envelopes: Used to _____ payments to office.

Tan Kraft: _____ envelopes, used for large documents.

Padded Envelopes: Used to send objects which may be otherwise _____ in transit.

Parts of a Business Letter:

Margin: Area around _____ of a form, blank. ____ _____ is standard.

Letterhead: Lists name, address, and phone number, usually at the _____ of the paper.

Dateline: Contains month, day, year. Begins _____ lines below letterhead, on _____. The month is always _____ ___, with a _____ after the day.

Inside Address: _____ and _____ of the person receiving the letter.

Key: Typing the address on the _____ margin, ____ spaces down from the date, ___ lines in length. Use a Courtesy Title, including the _____ _____. Numbers 1-9 are _____ _____, and anything over 10 is typed in _____. Spell out "Street", "Drive", etc. Use the _____ _____ _____ with the _____ _____ _____ _____. _____ space after state abbreviation, add _____ _____.

Attention Line: Used to send a letter to a _____ _____ in a company.

Salutation: " _____ X", followed by a colon.

Subject Line: Allows the reader to understand the subject of the letter. Placed on the second line _____ the salutation.

Body: _____ _____ below the salutation or subject.

Complimentary Closing: Placed two lines _____ the body. Example is "Sincerely".

Signature Block: First line is the _____ of the letter writer. Business title is placed on the _____ _____. Align with the _____ _____, four lines _____.

Identification Line: Writer's _____. Typed on the _____, two lines _____ the signature block.

Notations: _____ of enclosures included, _____ of others receiving a copy of the letter. Notations are placed on the _____ _____, one or two lines _____ the Identification Line.

Punctuation:

Open Punctuation: Uses _____ _____ with Attention, Salutation, Complimentary Closing, Signature Block, Enclosure, and Copy Notifications.

Mixed Punctuation: Uses a _____ after Attention and Salutation, a _____ after the Complimentary Closing, a _____ or _____ after the Enclosure Notation, and a _____ after the Copy Notation.

Letter Styles:

Full-Block Style: All lines flush _____.

Modified Block Style: Dateline, Complimentary Closing, Signature Block, and Notations aligned at the _____ of the page.

Simplified Style: _____ Salutation, Subject placed _____ the Address and Body, all text to the _____, ____ Complimentary Closing, sender's name and title in _____ on a single line at the ____ of the letter.

Address Placement: Address is bordered by a _____ _____ margin on the left and right, _____ margin on the bottom. The top of the city/state/zip code line should be no higher than _____ from the bottom.

Address Format: Type the address using _____ _____ _____ and _____ _____. The first line is the _____. The last line is the _____ _____ _____.

State Abbreviations:

Alabama: ___	Montana: ___
Alaska: ___	Nebraska: ___
Arizona: ___	Nevada: ___
Arkansas: ___	New Hampshire: ___
California: ___	New Jersey: ___
Colorado: ___	New Mexico: ___
Connecticut: ___	New York: ___
Delaware: ___	North Carolina: ___
Florida: ___	North Dakota: ___
Georgia: ___	Ohio: ___
Hawaii: ___	Oklahoma: ___
Idaho: ___	Oregon: ___
Illinois: ___	Pennsylvania: ___
Indiana: ___	Rhode Island: ___
Iowa: ___	South Carolina: ___
Kansas: ___	South Dakota: ___
Kentucky: ___	Tennessee: ___
Louisiana: ___	Texas: ___
Maine: ___	Utah: ___
Maryland: ___	Vermont: ___
Massachusetts: ___	Virginia: ___
Michigan: ___	Washington: ___
Minnesota: ___	Washington DC: ___
Mississippi: ___	West Virginia: ___
Missouri: ___	Wisconsin: ___
	Wyoming: ___

Financial Management

Omnibus Budget Reconciliation Act: Requires _____ _____ for Medicare based on a fee schedule.

Geographical Practice Cost Index: Adjusts _____ _____.

National Conversion Factor: Determines _____ _____ for all health care services.

Credit: Debt _____ to be paid by debtor at a later date.

Accounts Receivable: _____ owed to the office.

Collection: Acquiring _____ or _____ owed to the office.

Bankruptcy: Liquidation of _____ to repay debts.

Chapter 7 Bankruptcy: _____ are _____ _____ and funds distributed to creditors.

Chapter 13 Bankruptcy: Provides _____ to debtors who are in the process of arranging payments over three or five years.

Patient Billing Statement: Mailed once a month detailing _____ ____.

Collection Agency: Company used in order to collect _____ _____.

Fair Debt Collection Act: Prevents _____ or _____ collection practices.

Legal Knowledge

HIPAA: Health Insurance Accountability Act of 1996. Enacted August 21, 1996. Created by US Department of Heath and Human Services.

Title I: Health Care Portability. Allows persons to carry health insurance from one _____ to another _____.

Title II: _____ of Heath Care Fraud and Abuse, Administrative Simplification, and Medical Liability Reform.

Privacy Rule: Protects all individually _____ health information. Assures health information of individuals is _____ while allowing health information to be _____ between healthcare providers to provide high-quality health care.

    Individual's past, present, future physical or mental health or condition.

    Provision of health care to individual.

    Past, present, or future payment for provision of health care to individual.

Permitted Uses and Disclosures:

    To the individual.

    Treatment, Payment, Health Care Operations.

    Uses and Disclosures with Opportunity to Agree or Object

    Incidental Use and Disclosure.

    Public Interest and Benefit Activities.

    Limited Data Set.

Security Rule: Specifies _____ of patient _____ via computers and internet.

Title VII of the Civil Rights Act of 1964: Prevents _____ in the workplace or place of business.

Consent: Patient giving _____ for examination, treatment, or diagnoses.

Informed Consent: Right of patient to _____ and _____ all information related to their condition and treatment options.

Liability: Being _____ _____ for every aspect of a medical practice.

Malpractice: _____ in diagnosis or treatment.

Negligence: Failure of a medical professional to perform _____ _____ that result in _____ to a patient.

Confidentiality: Keeping patient information _____ and _____ at all times.

Code of Ethics: Guiding _____ _____ of right and wrong.

Types of Medical Businesses:

Sole Proprietorship: Medical practice owned by _____ _____.

Partnership: Medical practices owned by _____ or _____ persons.

Group Practice: Three or more physicians sharing income and expenses.

Professional Corporations: Authorized by state to act as a _____ _____.

Communication:

Body Language: _____ - _____ communication. Types include touch, eye contact, facial expressions, and posture.

Active Listening: Listening to the patient and _____ to statements being made.

Passive Listening: Listening to the patient _____ offering a reply.

Open Ended Question: Questions used when asking for _____ from patients.

Close Ended Question: Questions used that require only a _____ **or** _____ response.

Health Insurance

Group Health Benefits: Benefits offered by _____, _____, _____, or other _____.

Dependent: _____ or _____ covered by one person's insurance policy.

Deductible: Amount required to be paid by the _____-_____ before insurance payments begin.

Medicare: Provides health insurance to the _____, sponsored by the government.

Medicare Part A: Covers _____ expenses.

Medicare Part B: Covers physician _____, _____, _____ tests, and _____ tests.

Medicaid: Provides health insurance to _____-_____ _____. Regulated by both state and federal governments.

TRICARE: Provides health insurance for dependents of _____ military personnel, _____ military personnel, and dependents of _____ military personnel.

HMO: _____ of health care providers who have contracted with the health insurer.

PPO: Preferred Provider Organization. List of providers _____ to health care plans.

Coding

ICD-9-CM: DX coding system used to code _____.

E Codes: Used for classifying cause of _____, _____, or adverse _____ reactions.

M Codes: Used by _____ registries to identify _____ and _____.

V Codes: Used to describe circumstances other than _____ or _____. Examples include preventative care, chemotherapy, or radiation therapy.

CMS-1500: Used to document up to _____ different conditions.

CPT: Coding system used to document _____. CPT manual contains ____ sections.

Complete
Study
Guide

Medical Terminology

Medical terminology is widely used throughout the medical field, and is the primary way of communicating with other health-care professionals. Medical terminology has origins in Latin and Greek. A medical term consists of three parts: The word root, which is what the term is mainly talking about; the prefix, which comes at the beginning of the medical term; the suffix, which comes at the end of the word. Both the prefix and suffix help to further describe what may be happening in a certain medical condition.

Word Roots

Abdomin/o: Abdomen
Acr/o: Extremity
Aden/o: Gland
Adip/o: Fat
Angi/o: Vessel
Ankyl/o: Bent, crooked
Arteri/o: Artery
Arthr/o: Joint
Ather/o: Fatty plaque
Audi/o: Hearing
Aur/o: Ear
Bi/o: Life
Brachi/o: Arm

Bucc/o: Cheek
Carcin/o: Cancer
Cardi/o: Heart
Cephal/o: Head
Chlor/o: Green
Chol/e: Bile
Cholecyst/o: Gallbladder
Chondr/o: Cartilage
Cirrh/o: Yellow
Col/o: Large intestine
Corp/o: Body
Cost/o: Ribs
Cry/o: Cold

Cutane/o: Skin

Cyan/o: Blue

Cyst/o: Bladder

Dent/o: Teeth

Derm/o: Skin

Dist/o: Far

Dors/o: Back

Embol/o: Plug

Emphys/o: Inflate

Encephal/o: Brain

Enter/o: Small Intestine

Erythr/o: Red

Esophag/o: Esophagus

Gastr/o: Stomach

Gingiv/o: Gums

Gloss/o: Tongue

Gluc/o: Sugar

Hem/o: Blood

Hepat/o: Liver

Hist/o: Tissue

Home/o: Same

Hydr/o: Water

Hyster/o: Uterus

Inguin/o: Groin

Jaund/o: Yellow

Kerat/o: Hard

Kinesi/o: Movement

Kyph/o: Hill

Lact/o: Milk

Later/o: Side

Leuk/o: White

Lip/o: Fat

Lord/o: Curve

Mamm/o: Breast

Mast/o: Breast

Melan/o: Black

My/o: Muscle

Myel/o: Canal

Nas/o: Nose

Necr/o: Death

Nephr/o: Kidney

Neur/o: Nerve

Ocul/o: Eye

Onc/o: Tumor

Oophor/o: Ovary

Oste/o: Bone

Path/o: Disease

Ped/o: Foot

Phleb/o: Vein

Phren/o: Diaphragm

Pneum/o: Lung

Proxim/o: Near

Pulm/o: Lung

Pyr/o: Heat

Ren/o: Kidney

Rhin/o: Nose

Salping/o: Fallopian tube

Scler/o: Hard

Scoli/o: Crooked

Somat/o: Body

Spondyl/o: Vertebrae

Stomat/o: Mouth

Thorac/o: Chest

Ventr/o: Belly

Prefixes

a-: Without
ab-: Away from
ad-: Towards
af-: Towards
an-: Without
ana-: Against
ante-: Before
anti-: Against
auto-: Self
bi-: Two
brady-: Slow
circum-: Around
contra-: Against
di-: Double
dia-: Through
dys-: Bad, difficult
ef-: Away from
endo-: In
epi-: Above
exo-: Outside
homeo-: Same
hyper-: Excessive
hypo-: Below
infra-: Under

inter-: Between
intra-: Inside
iso-: Same
macro-: Large
mal-: Bad
meta-: Change
micro-: Small
mono-: One
multi-: Many
neo-: New
pan-: All
para-: Near
peri-: Around
poly-: Many
post-: After
pre-: Before
pseudo-: False
quadri-: Four
retro-: Behind
supra-: Above
syn-: Together
tachy-: Rapid
tri-: Three
uni-: One

Suffixes

-ac: Pertaining to
-al: Pertaining to
-algia: Pain
-ar: Pertaining to
-blast: Germ cell
-cision: Cutting
-clast: Break
-crine: Secrete
-cyte: Cell
-derma: Skin
-ectomy: Removal
-edema: Swelling
-emia: Blood condition
-esis: Condition
-ferent: To carry
-gen: Formation
-globin: Protein
-ic: Pertaining to
-ician: Specialist
-icle: Small

-ist: Specialist
-itis: Inflammation
-lysis: Dissolve
-oid: Resembling
-osis: Condition
-pathy: Disease
-phagia: Eating
-phasia: Speech
-physis: Growth
-plasia: Formation
-plegia: Paralysis
-pnea: Breathing
-poiesis: Formation
-rrhage: Bursting forth
-rrhea: Discharge
-stasis: Standing still
-tomy: Incision
-trophy: Nourishment
-uria: Urine

Anatomy and Physiology

Anatomy: The study of the **structure** of the human body.

Systemic Anatomy: The study of the body's **organ systems.**

Regional Anatomy: The study of the different **regions** of the body.

Physiology: The study of the **function** of the human body.

Cells: Cells are the functional units of all tissues, and they perform all essential life functions.

Cellular Mitosis: A cell **dividing** from one mother cell into two daughter cells in order to replace cell loss.

Organelles are found **inside** cells to make the cells function.

Nucleus: Contains **DNA**, controls activity inside cells.

Nucleolus: Forms **ribosomes** and **synthesizes RNA** in ribosomes.

Mitochondria: Produce **ATP.**

Golgi Apparatus: Allows **transportation of protein** in cells.

Smooth Endoplasmic Reticulum: Synthesizes **carbohydrates** and **lipids.**

Lysosome: Break down protein inside cells.

Ribosome: Contain **RNA and protein**, assemble cell proteins.

Cytoplasm: Gel-like substance inside cell.

Homeostasis: Homeostasis is the existence and maintenance of a **constant internal environment.** Several factors contribute to the homeostatic process, including hormones, nerve impulses, and sweating.

Homeostatic Mechanisms: Homeostatic mechanisms are **physical** things that happen in the body that alter the internal environment in response to a specific change. **Sweating** reduces body temperature, and **shivering** increases body temperature.

REGIONAL ANATOMY

There are three main regions of the body:

Central
Upper Limb
Lower Limb

Central Body Region

Central Body Region: The Central body region contains everything in the center of the body, such as the **head, neck, and trunk.** The trunk can be further divided into three other regions:

Thorax: The thorax(thoracic) contains our major internal organs, such as the **heart and lungs.** Also inside the thorax is the **mediastinum**, a form of connective tissue that surrounds organs inside the chest(except the lungs), protecting them from too much jostling.

Abdomen: The abdomen contains the majority of our digestive organs, including the stomach, liver, gallbladder, pancreas, small intestine, large intestine, kidneys, and spleen.

Pelvis: The pelvis contains our **internal reproductive organs**, the **descending and sigmoid colons**, and the **urinary bladder.**

Body Cavities

Body Cavities: Body cavities **hold things inside them.** There are two main body cavities:

Dorsal Body Cavity: Made by the **skull and vertebral column**, contains the **brain and spinal cord.**

Ventral Body Cavity: Made by the three trunk cavities(**thorax, abdomen, pelvis**).

Directional Terms

Directional Terms: Used to describe structures in the body in relation to other structures or body parts.

Superior: Above
Inferior: Below
Anterior: Front
Posterior: Back
Proximal: Closer to the midline

Distal: Further from the midline
Medial: Middle
Lateral: Side
Deep: More internal
Superficial: Towards the surface

Body Planes: There are **four main planes** used to divide the body.
Sagittal: Splits the body into **left and right.**
Midsagittal: Splits the body into **equal left and right sides**, runs down the **midline** of the body.
Transverse/Horizontal: Splits the body into **superior and inferior.**
Frontal/Coronal: Splits the body into **anterior and posterior.**

TISSUE

There are **four** types of tissue in the human body:
Epithelial, Nervous, Muscular, and Connective.

Epithelial: Forms most **glands**, the **digestive tract**, and the **epidermis.**
Epithelial tissue is responsible for **protecting** the body, **absorbing** nutrients, and **secreting** substances. Epithelial tissue is **avascular** and contains no blood vessels.

Nervous: Forms the **brain, spinal cord,** and **nerves** that emerge from
both. Nervous tissue allows for **sensation, mental activity,** and **movement** of skeletal muscle.
A **neuron** is a **nerve cell**. It contains a **nucleus**, the site of cell function. It also contains **dendrites**, branch-like projections that come off the cell body to receive nervous impulses, bringing them into the cell body.

Muscular: There are three types of muscle: **Skeletal, cardiac, smooth.**
Skeletal: Connects to the **skeleton** and allows **voluntary movements**.
Cardiac: Muscle of the **heart,** responsible for **pumping blood** throughout the body.
Smooth: Found in locations such as the **skin**(arrector pili) and **digestive**

tract. Responsible for actions such as **peristalsis**.

Connective: Connective tissue is formed by the "extracellular matrix",

materials you don't find in cells. They can contain **protein**, **non-fibrous protein**, and **fluid**. Connective tissue is responsible for actions such as **separating** structures, **connecting** structures, **transportation** of nutrients, **cushioning** and **insulating** the body, and **protecting** the body.
Blast Cells: Immature cells that **build** the matrix.
Clast Cells: **Break down** the matrix.
There are several types of connective tissue, including **bone**, **cartilage**, **tendons**, **ligaments**, **adipose**, **fascia**, **serous membranes**, and **blood**. The most abundant form of connective tissue in the body is **blood**.

Blood: Consists of **erythrocytes**, **leukocytes**, **thrombocytes**, and **plasma**.
Erythrocytes: Also called **red blood cells**, responsible for **transporting** oxygen and carbon dioxide throughout the body via **hemoglobin**, which is found in the cytoplasm of the cells.
Leukocytes: Also called **white blood cells**, they are **phagocytes** that help fight off infectious agents and break down dead cells and debris inside the body.
Thrombocytes: Also called **platelets**, they are responsible for **clotting** the blood.
Plasma: The **liquid** portion of blood, allows **transportation** of blood cells throughout the body.

Serous Membranes: Forms of connective tissues that **surround** organs inside body cavities, preventing the organs from creating friction. There are **two** serous membranes inside the **thorax**: the **pericardium**, which surrounds the **heart**, and the **pleura**, which surrounds the **lungs**. There is **one** serous membrane that is found inside the **abdomen** and **pelvis** that separates the organs from the muscle on top of them: the **peritoneum**.
Inner wall of a serous membrane: **Visceral** serous membrane
Outer wall of a serous membrane: **Parietal** serous membrane

BODY SYSTEMS

Cardiovascular System: Responsible for **transporting blood** throughout the body, bringing oxygen, hormones, and nutrients to tissues, and eliminating carbon dioxide and waste products from the body. Consists of the **heart**, **blood vessels**, and **blood**.

Heart: Pumps blood throughout the body. Consists of the superior vena cava, inferior vena cava, right atrium, tricuspid valve, right ventricle, pulmonary valve, pulmonary arteries, pulmonary veins, left atrium, bicuspid valve, left ventricle, aortic valve, and aorta.

Blood Vessels: Create **passageways** for blood to travel throughout the body.

Arteries: Largest and most internal blood vessels, move blood **away from the heart**, and almost always carry oxygenated blood.

Veins: Move blood **towards the heart,** and almost always carry deoxygenated blood.

Capillaries: Microscopic blood vessels used to transport oxygen-rich blood **into tissues**.

Pathologies of the Cardiovascular System:

Anemia: Decrease in **oxygen-carrying** ability of the blood, most commonly due to a lack of **erythrocytes**, **hemoglobin**, or both. Causes fatigue due to **hypoxia**.

Aneurysm: Bulging of a wall of an artery outward, caused by a **weakened** arterial wall. Most likely the result of **hypertension** putting strain on the arterial wall. May break open, resulting in severe **hemorrhaging** internally, which may be fatal.

Angina Pectoris: Pain in the **chest** resulting from myocardial ischemia. Pain may also radiate into the **left arm**.

Arteriosclerosis: Hardening of the walls of arteries, caused by a lack of elasticity in the arteries. Reduces circulation, which may lead to **hypertension**.

Atherosclerosis: Buildup of **fatty plaque**, or **lipids**, on the walls of the arteries, reducing blood flow. May result in **hypertension** and the formation of **blood clots**.

Embolism: A **blood clot** or **bubble of gas** freely moving throughout the circulatory system. May become lodged in the heart, lungs, or brain, resulting in lack of blood flow to those structures, causing **necrosis**.

Endocarditis: Inflammation of the **inner lining** of the heart as a result of infection.

Heart Murmur: Flow of blood **backwards** in the heart due to malfunctioning **valves**, typically the bicuspid or mitral valve. Formation of **blood clots** may occur, along with fatigue.

Hypertension: High blood pressure, 140/90 mm Hg. Results in inelasticity of the arterial walls, reducing circulation.

Migraine: Vascular headache. Caused by **dilation** of extracranial blood vessels, which puts substantial pressure upon the **meninges**, producing intense pain. May be caused by stress or smoke, among other things.

Myocardial Infarction: Death of **heart tissue**, usually caused by a blockage in the **coronary arteries**, which are responsible for supplying the myocardium with blood.

Pericarditis: Inflammation of the **pericardium**, usually the result of an infectious disease.

Phlebitis: Inflammation of a **vein**, caused by trauma, pregnancy, prolonged periods of sitting or standing, and may present with **blood clots**.

Raynaud's Syndrome: Constriction of **blood vessels** in the **hands and feet**, which reduces blood supply. Caused by cigarette smoking, cold exposure, or stress.

Transient Ischemic Attack: Temporary **cerebral** dysfunction resulting from **ischemia** in part of the brain. Also known as a **"mini-stroke"**, it can be a precursor to a more serious stroke in the future.

Varicose Veins: Swollen veins, caused by dysfunction in the **valves** inside the veins, resulting in blood pooling down the legs and forcing the veins towards the surface of the body.

Digestive System:
Responsible for bringing food **into the body**, **digestion**, **absorption** of nutrients, and **elimination** of waste.

Oral Cavity: Also called the **mouth**, contains the **teeth**, **salivary glands**, and **tongue**. Performs **mastication** and **swallowing**.

Pharynx: Also called the **throat**, allows **transport** of food from the oral cavity to the esophagus.

Esophagus: Tubular organ that allows **transport** of food from the pharynx to the stomach.

Stomach: Digests and **breaks down** food into usable, absorbable nutrients.

Liver: Filters harmful chemicals from the blood, produces **bile**.

Gallbladder: Stores bile and **empties bile** into the duodenum.

Pancreas: Produces **insulin** and **glucagon** and secretes these substances into the duodenum.

Small Intestine: Absorbs nutrients into the body for use. Consists of the **duodenum, jejunum,** and **ileum**.

Large Intestine: Absorbs water, converts chyme to **feces**, assists in **elimination** of waste.

Between organs in the Digestive System, we have **sphincters**. Sphincters are **ring-like** bands of **muscle** that allow food to pass through into other organs, and to **prevent** food from going **backwards** in the digestive tract. There are four main sphincters in the digestive tract:

Esophageal Sphincter: Located between the **pharynx** and **esophagus**.

Cardiac Sphincter: Located between the **esophagus** and **stomach**.

Pyloric Sphincter: Located between the **stomach** and **small intestine**.

Ileocecal Sphincter: Located between the **small intestine** and **large intestine**.

Pathologies of the Digestive System:

Cholecystitis: Inflammation of the **gallbladder**, usually due to a blockage of the **cystic duct**, stopping the flow of **bile** into the duodenum. Blockages most commonly caused by **gallstones**.

Cirrhosis: Destruction of **liver** cells, resulting in the formation of adhesions and fibrous material in the **liver**, causing the **liver** to become a yellowish-orange color. **Liver** function is gradually impaired.

Crohn's Disease: Autoimmune disorder which affects the **gastrointestinal** tract, resulting in **inflammation** and **ulceration** of the mucous membranes, in which scar tissue can develop.

Diverticulosis: Development of small **pouches** that protrude from the walls of the **large intestine**, caused by weakening of the walls due to a lack of substances for the walls to press against.

Diverticulitis: Inflammation of **diverticular pouches**, which may become abscessed and develop ulcers.

Gastroenteritis: Inflammation of the **lining of the stomach** and **small intestine**, most commonly caused by food poisoning or emotional stress.

Gastroesophageal Reflux Disease: Hydrochloric acid flowing from the **stomach** upwards **into the esophagus**, producing a burning sensation. May result in ulcers in the esophagus.

Hepatitis: Inflammation of the **liver** most commonly associated with a **viral infection**, which may be acute or chronic. Results in pain, nausea, fatigue, diarrhea, and jaundice in the acute stage of infection.

Hernia: Protrusion of an organ through the surrounding connective tissue membrane. May result in pain and impaired body function, depending on the location and herniated structures involved.

Ulcerative Colitis: Autoimmune disorder resulting in **inflammation** of the **walls of the large intestine**, producing ulcerations. May result in bloody stools, diarrhea, and weight loss.

<u>Endocrine System</u>: Responsible for **coordinating** the specific activities of cells and tissues via **hormone** release. Endocrine glands secrete hormones directly into the **blood stream**.

Pineal Gland: Secretes **melatonin**. The exact role of the pineal gland is unknown.

Pituitary Gland: Secretes **growth hormone, prolactin**, and **follicle-stimulating** hormones. Responsible for **growth** in bones, production of **milk**, and production of **egg** cells in women and **sperm** cells in men.

Thyroid: Secretes **thyroxine** and **triiodothyronine**, responsible for increasing **energy** production.

Parathyroids: Secrete **parathyroid** hormone, which raises concentration of **calcium** in the blood.

Adrenals: Secrete **epinephrine** and **norepinephrine**, which elevate **blood pressure**, increase **heart rate**, and increase **blood sugar**.

Pancreatic Islets: Secrete **insulin** and **glucagon**. Insulin **lowers** glucose concentration in the blood, while glucagon **increases** glucose concentration in the blood.

Ovaries: Secrete **estrogen** and **progesterone**.

Testes: Secrete **testosterone**.

Pathologies of the Endocrine System:

Addison's Disease: Autoimmune disorder which results in the **degeneration** of the **adrenal cortex**, causing a decrease in adrenal function.

Cushing's Disease: Over-production of **corticosteroids**, resulting in increased weight and muscle atrophy.

Diabetes Mellitus: Increased levels of **glucose** in the blood stream. Diabetes Type I is caused by a **decrease** in **insulin levels** in the body, which restricts the breaking down of glucose, while Diabetes Type II is caused by the body being **desensitized** to **insulin**, which is then unable to break down glucose.

Goiter: Enlargement of the **thyroid gland**, commonly seen with hyperthyroidism, hypothyroidism, inflammation, or a lack of **iodine** in the diet.

Grave's Disease: Autoimmune disease resulting in **hyperthyroidism**, anxiety, trembling, and fatigue. May also result in protrusion of the eyeballs.

Hyperthyroidism: Increased **thyroid** function, results in a **goiter**, hypersensitivity to heat, increased appetite, and increased respiration.

Hypothyroidism: Lack of **thyroid** hormone in the body, results in fatigue, weight gain, edema, and sensitivity to cold.

<u>Integumentary System</u>: Contains the **skin, hair, nails, sweat glands, oil glands**, and **sensory receptors**. Responsible for **protection**, **secretion** of substances, **absorption** of substances, and detecting **sensation**.

Skin: Made of epithelial tissue, skin is avascular and is used for **protection**.

Sudoriferous Glands: Secrete **sweat**, which is a homeostatic mechanism. Sudoriferous glands are forms of exocrine glands.

Sebaceous Glands: Secrete **oil**. Sebaceous glands are forms of exocrine glands.

Sensory Receptors: Detect **sensation** in the skin.

Pacinian Corpuscles: Detect **deep** pressure.

Meissner's Corpuscles: Detect **light** pressure.

Thermoreceptors: Detect differentiations in **temperature**.

Nociceptors: Detect **pain.**

Pathologies of the Integumentary System:

Acne: Bacterial infection of the skin, due to numerous factors, including **testosterone** production, stress, and hormonal imbalance.

Athlete's Foot: Also called **Tinea Pedis**, it is a highly contagious **fungal** infection found on the feet, primarily between the toes, which may result in breaking of the skin and lead to bacterial infection.

Basal Cell Carcinoma: Least serious, **slowest** growing, **most** common form of skin cancer, usually due to overexposure to sunlight.

Burns: First degree burn – Most common, least serious. Most common form is a sunburn, affecting the **epidermis**, resulting in inflammation and irritation of the skin.

Second degree burn – Burn moves **through** the **epidermis** into the **dermis**, which leads to the development of **blisters** and swelling.

Third degree burn – Burn moves **through** the **epidermis** and the **dermis**, into the **subcutaneous layer**. Results in **necrosis** and scarring of the skin, and may lead to infection if not treated properly.

Cellulitis: Acute infection caused by **staphylococci** or **streptococci** bacteria, which often enters the body through exposure to **wounds**, affecting nearby tissues. Presents with well-defined borders of inflammation.

Decubitus Ulcer: Also known as a **pressure ulcer** or **bed sore**, results in **ulcerations** caused by prolonged **pressure** placed on a part of the body, causing **ischemia** and ultimately **necrosis** of the affected tissue.

Eczema: Idiopathic disorder causing **dry, red, itchy patches** of skin. May be either acute or chronic.

Herpes Simplex: Highly contagious chronic **viral** infection, resulting in **cold sores** around the mucous membranes.

Hives: Also known as **urticaria**, it is an inflammatory reaction in response to exposure to an **allergen** or **emotional stress**. May be either acute or chronic, depending on the cause.

Impetigo: Acute **bacterial** infection caused by staphylococci or streptococci, results in sores that form around the mouth, nose, and hands. Mostly seen in **children**, it is highly contagious.

Lice: Highly contagious **parasitic** infection, found in hair. Produce egg sacs called "nits".

Malignant Melanoma: Over-production of **melanocytes**, resulting in formation of tumors that may spread to other regions of the body. A = Asymmetrical, B = Border, C = Color, D = Diameter, E = Elevated.

Mole: Benign skin lesion, resulting from an increased amount of **melanin** in an area.

Psoriasis: Autoimmune disorder in which the body's immune system attacks **epithelial** tissue. Epithelial cells quickly regenerate at a rate quicker than normal, which results in **thick, dry, silvery** patches of skin.

Ringworm: Also known as **Tinea Corporis**, it is a **fungal** infection resulting in circular raised patches on the skin.

Rosacea: A form of **acne**, results in a **butterfly rash** that appears across the nose and cheeks. Exacerbated by exposure to cold.

Scleroderma: An autoimmune disorder, resulting in excessive **collagen** production in the skin, causing the skin to become **hardened**. Can be a sign of organ failure.

Sebaceous Cyst: Blockage of a **sebaceous gland**, resulting in the body forming a thick membrane of connective tissue around the gland, limiting tissue damage as a result of infection.

Squamous Cell Carcinoma: Form of skin cancer which develops into an area of **ulceration**, caused by overexposure to sunlight, or may be found in the mouth of a person who chews tobacco or smokes cigarettes.

Wart: Epidermal protrusion resulting from infection by the **Human Papilloma Virus**. Results in increased **keratin** production on the area of infection.

Lymphatic System: Consists of **lymph nodes, lymph vessels, lymph,** and **lymph organs**.

Lymph Vessels: They are a **one-way** system, meaning lymph in the vessels only flows one direction. The vessels **absorb** foreign bodies and nutrients from tissue.

Lymph Nodes: A lymph node is a **mass** of lymph tissue, responsible for **filtering** and **destroying** foreign objects, helps to **produce antibodies**.

Lymph: Made of mostly water, protein, leukocytes, urea, salts, and glucose.

Spleen: Removes old **red blood cells** from the blood stream.

Thymus: Produces **T-lymphocytes**(T-cells).

Pathologies of the Lymphatic System:

Acquired Immunodeficiency Syndrome: Immune disorder caused by **HIV**, which destroys the body's **T-cells**, effectively disabling the immune system.

Allergies: Hypersensitivity of the body to agents which are normally harmless in most people.

Chronic Fatigue Syndrome: Idiopathic disease which results in symptoms such as **insomnia**, **low-grade fever**, and **irritability**.

Lymphedema: Increased amounts of **interstitial fluid** in a limb, resulting in **swelling**. Caused by inflammation, trauma, or blocked lymph channels.

Lupus: Autoimmune disorder affecting the **connective tissues** of the body, resulting in a rash across the face, scales on the skin, fatigue, fever, photo-sensitivity, and weight loss.

Mononucleosis: Viral infection, resulting in a high fever, fatigue, sore throat, and swollen lymph nodes.

Pitting Edema: Swollen area, leaves **pits** in the skin after applying pressure. May be a sign of **organ failure**.

<u>Muscular System</u>: Contains **muscles**. Muscles are responsible for **movement** and **creating heat.**

In order for a muscle to contract, **calcium** must be present. The contractile unit of a muscle is called a **sarcomere**. Sarcomeres are formed by **thin** filaments(**actin**) and **thick** filaments(**myosin**).

Muscle Contractions: A contraction is when **tension** in a muscle **increases**.

Isometric Contraction: The **length** of a muscle **stays the same**, but **tension** in the muscle **increases**.

Isotonic Contraction: The **tension** in a muscle **stays the same**, but the **length** of the muscle **changes**.

Concentric Contraction: The **tension** in a muscle **increases**, and muscle **length decreases**.

Eccentric Contraction: The **tension** in the muscle **stays the same**, and muscle **length increases**.

Prime Mover/Agonist: The muscle of a synergist group **responsible for movement**.

Synergist: A muscle that **assists** the prime mover in performing the action.

Antagonist: A muscle that **opposes** the prime mover, performing the **opposite** action.

Fixator: A muscle that **stabilizes** an area so an action can be performed.

Pathologies of the Muscular System:

Adhesive Capsulitis: Formation of **adhesions** that stick the **joint capsule** to the head of the **humerus**, severely restricting the range of motion at the shoulder joint. May also be caused by hypertonicity of the subscapularis.

Atrophy: Loss of **muscle density** due to lack of use or malnourishment.

Drop Foot: Paralysis or severe weakness of the **tibialis anterior**, placing the ankle into forced **plantarflexion**. May also be caused by hypertonicity of the gastrocnemius.

Fibromyalgia: Inflammatory disease affecting muscles and connective tissue, resulting in **pain**, numbness, tingling sensations in the limbs, and fatigue.

Golfer's Elbow: A form of **tendonitis**, results in inflammation and pain located at the **medial epicondyle of the humerus**. The **flexors** of the wrist are affected, as they originate on the medial epicondyle of the humerus.

Muscular Dystrophy: Autoimmune disorder, resulting in **degeneration** of muscles. Muscle degeneration leads to **atrophy** and lack of use, eventually resulting in paralysis and deformity.

Strain: An injury to a **muscle** or **tendon**, may be caused by overexertion or overstretching.

Temporomandibular Joint Dysfunction: Pain in the **jaw** upon opening and closing, **clicking** at the temporomandibular joint, and decreased range of motion. Results from trauma to the joint or muscles, clenching of the teeth, grinding of the teeth, stress, or a combination of the previous causes.

Tendonitis: Inflammation of a **tendon**, results from injury to either the tenoperiosteal or musculotendinous junction.

Tennis Elbow: A common form of **tendonitis**, results in inflammation and pain located at the **lateral epicondyle of the humerus**. The **extensors** of the wrist are affected, as they originate at the lateral epicondyle of the humerus.

Torticollis: Spasm of the **sternocleidomastoid** unilaterally, forcing the head to lean to **one side**. **Vertigo** may result.

Whiplash: Straining or spraining of tendons, muscles, and ligaments in the **neck** due to violent **forward** motion of the head and neck. As a result, tendons, muscles and ligaments may be injured and weakened, with an increase in headaches, pain, and dizziness. Most commonly seen in **automobile accidents**.

Nervous System: There are two branches of the Nervous System, the **Central Nervous System** and **Peripheral Nervous System**. It also contains the **Autonomic Nervous System.**

Central Nervous System: Consists of the **brain** and **spinal cord**.
Brain: Consists of the **cerebrum, cerebellum**, and **brain stem.**
Cerebrum: The **largest** part of the brain, split into left and right **hemispheres**, responsible for **voluntary** actions and **sensory** reception. Each hemisphere contains **lobes**, named after bones overlaying them.

Frontal Lobe: Responsible for **voluntary** motor function, **motivation, aggression, mood**.
Parietal Lobe: Responsible for processing most **sensory** information.
Temporal Lobe: Responsible for **auditory** and **olfactory** processing, and **memory**.
Occipital Lobe: Responsible for **visual** input.

Cerebellum: Responsible for **muscle tone, coordination**, and **balance**.
Brain Stem: Contains three parts: **Medulla Oblongata, Pons**, and **Midbrain**.
Medulla Oblongata: Regulates the body's **vital functions**.
Pons: Creates a pathway for **communication** between the **cerebrum** and **cerebellum**.
Midbrain: **Visual reflexes**.
Peripheral Nervous System: Contains **nerves**. There are **31 pairs** of **spinal nerves** that emerge from the spinal cord, and **12 pairs** of **cranial nerves** that emerge from the brain.
Cranial Nerves: Emerge from the brain, numbered via Roman numerals. Olfactory(I), Optic(II), Oculomotor(III), Trochlear(IV), Trigeminal(V), Abducent(VI), Facial(VII), Vestibulocochlear(VIII), Hypoglossal(IX), Vagus(X), Spinal Accessory(XI), Glossopharyngeal(XII)

Autonomic Nervous System: Responsible for maintenance of **homeostasis** within the body. There are two autonomic nervous responses in the body.
Sympathetic Response: Also called "**fight-or-flight**", when activated, increases **norepinephrine** in the body, **increasing** heart rate. It also **shuts down** digestive organs and pulls blood from them for use in the muscles.
Parasympathetic Response: Also called "**rest-and-digest**", when activated, **decreases** heart rate, brings blood into the digestive organs to stimulate **peristalsis**. Controlled by Cranial Nerve X, the **Vagus Nerve**.

Pathologies of the Nervous System:

Alzheimer's Disease: Progressive **degeneration** of **brain tissue**, resulting in loss of memory, dementia, confusion and disorientation.

Bell's Palsy: Paralysis of **one side of the face** as a result of inflammation or compression of the facial nerve. May be permanent, or may subside.

Carpal Tunnel Syndrome: Compression of the **median nerve** by the transverse carpal ligament, resulting in loss of function and sensation in the hand.

Cerebral Palsy: Loss of muscle control and coordination due to **damage** to certain parts of the **brain** during early life stages such as infancy.

Encephalitis: Inflammation of the **brain**, most commonly caused by a **viral** infection. The virus usually enters the body after contact with **mosquitoes**. Inflammation may result in necrotic brain tissue and death.

Hemiplegia: Paralysis of **one side** of the body, usually as the result of a **stroke**, which may impair function to specific regions of the body.

Meningitis: Inflammation of the **meninges**. **Bacterial** meningitis is the most severe form, which may result in death. Symptoms include nausea, vomiting, dizziness, and headache. Highly contagious.

Multiple Sclerosis: Autoimmune disorder in which the immune system attacks the **myelin sheaths** surrounding axons in the central nervous system, causing degeneration of the myelin. Degeneration also results in scarring on the axons, which results in severe pain in acute stages.

Paraplegia: Paralysis of the **lower limbs** due to an injury to the spinal cord anywhere below the T1 segment. Loss of function results in muscle atrophy.

Parkinson's Disease: Shaking or **trembling** due to reduced levels of the neurotransmitter **dopamine** in the body. Affects fine motor movements at first, then affects larger movements as the disease advances.

Quadriplegia: Paralysis of the **arms and legs**, resulting from an injury to the spinal cord between C5 and T1.

Sciatica: Compression of the **sciatic nerve** by hypertonic muscles, most commonly the **piriformis**. Results in pain radiating down the leg, and may even reach the bottoms of the feet.

Trigeminal Neuralgia: Compression of the **trigeminal nerve**, resulting in **severe pain** around the mouth, nose, and eyes.

Reproductive System: The reproductive system is divided into two
subcategories, **Male Reproductive System** and **Female Reproductive System.**
Male Reproductive System: Produces **spermatozoa** and **male hormones**. Consists of the **penis, testes, scrotum,** and **ducts** that carry sperm.
Penis: Responsible for **sexual intercourse**, allowing passage of sperm and urine out of the body.
Testes: Found inside the scrotum, responsible for **production** of **spermatozoa** and **testosterone**. Attach to the urethra via the **vas deferens.**
Female Reproductive System: Produce **egg cells, estrogen**, and development of a **fetus**. Consists of the **vagina, uterus, fallopian tubes,** and **ovaries**.
Vagina: Located between the cervix and the opening to the outside of the body. Allows a **passageway** for the penis during **intercourse**.
Ovaries: Glands that produce **oocytes**, or egg cells, and **estrogen**.
Fallopian Tubes: Allow **passage** of an oocyte from the ovaries to the uterus. **Fertilization** most often occurs in the fallopian tubes.

Respiratory System: Exchanges **oxygen** and **carbon dioxide** in blood,
and aids in **eliminating waste** from the body.
Nose: Conducts and **warms air** coming in and exiting the body. **Filters** air via **mucous.**
Larynx: Tube at front of pharynx, strengthened by muscles. Contains the **epiglottis**, which prevents food from entering the larynx during swallowing. Allows **speech.**
Trachea: Cartilage inferior to the larynx, allows **passage of air** into lungs.
Bronchi: Split into right and left, divides into smaller branches as they move through the lungs. Smallest branches are called **bronchioles**. They secrete **mucous** to trap dirt and debris, which is then expelled from the lungs by

cilia.

Alveoli: Air sacs at the end of bronchial tubes, connect to blood vessels. Responsible for **exchange** of oxygen and carbon dioxide.

Diaphragm: Muscle attached to base of rib cage and vertebrae, creates a vacuum to **bring air into the lungs** and **expel air from the lungs.** When the diaphragm **descends**, air **enters** the lungs. When the diaphragm **ascends**, air **exits** the lungs.

Pathologies of the Respiratory System:

Apnea: Cessation of breathing, temporarily. Most commonly occurs during **sleep**, commonly caused by compression of airways by the tongue or pharynx.

Asthma: Spasm of **smooth muscle** in the bronchial tubes, which is a reaction to stimuli such as **allergens** or **emotional stress**. Mucous production is also increased, further reducing air intake, creating wheezing sounds upon inhalation.

Bronchitis: Inflammation of **bronchial tubes**, with additional mucous production. **Acute** bronchitis is the side effect of a **primary infection** such as influenza, while **chronic** bronchitis is the result of irritants entering the lungs over a long period of time, such as **cigarette smoke**.

Cystic Fibrosis: Genetic disorder producing **thick mucous** throughout the respiratory tract, reducing air intake. Mucous blocks the **cystic duct**, limiting absorption of nutrients.

Emphysema: Destruction of lung **alveoli** due to exposure to irritants such as **cigarette smoke**, reducing oxygen intake and carbon dioxide output.

Influenza: Acute **viral** infection, resulting in an inflamed pharynx and nasal cavity, increased mucous production, and fever.

Laryngitis: Inflammation of the **larynx** resulting in **loss of voice**. Most commonly caused by an infection, but can be caused by cigarette smoke.

Pleurisy: Inflammation of **pleural membranes** surrounding lungs, resulting in a **burning sensation** upon inhalation.

Pneumonia: Streptococcal infection in the lungs, which fills the lung alveoli with fluid and waste products, reducing air intake.

Skeletal System: Contains **bones.** Responsible for **protecting** the body, **creating blood cells,** providing **structure,** and giving muscles a **location to attach to** which **permits movement.**

Axial Skeleton: Consists of the **skull, vertebral column,** and **thoracic cage.**

Skull: Protects the brain. Contains the following bones: Frontal, occipital, parietal, temporal, mandible, maxilla, sphenoid, vomer, nasal, ethmoid, lacrimal, and zygomatic.

There are four main sutures of the cranium, holding the bones of the skull together. They are:

Sagittal Suture: Connects the two **parietal bones.**

Coronal Suture: Connects the **frontal bone** to the **parietal bones.**

Squamous Suture: Connects the **temporal bone** and **parietal bone.**

Lambdoid Suture: Connects the **occipital bone** and the **parietal bones.**

Vertebral Column: Protects the spinal cord. Contains **26** individual bones. **Seven cervical** vertebrae, **twelve thoracic** vertebrae, **five lumbar** vertebrae, **one sacral** vertebrae, **one coccygeal** vertebrae.

Thoracic Cage: Also called the **rib cage, protects** the organs inside the thorax. There are **twelve pairs** of ribs. The **superior seven** pairs are called **true ribs.** The **inferior five** pairs are called **false ribs. Ribs 11 and 12** are called **floating ribs,** and they do not attach to the sternum.

Appendicular Skeleton: Consists of the bones of the **upper** and **lower limbs,** and the **pectoral** and **pelvic girdles.**

Upper Limb: Contains the humerus, radius, ulna, carpals, metacarpals, and phalanges.

Carpals: Scaphoid, Lunate, Triquetrum, Pisiform, Trapezium, Trapezoid, Capitate, Hamate.

Lower Limb: Contains the femur, tibia, fibula, tarsals, metatarsals, and phalanges.

Tarsals: Calcaneus, Cuboid, Cuneiform I, Cuneiform II, Cuneiform III, Talus, Navicular.

Pectoral Girdle: Contains the clavicles and scapulae.

Pelvic Girdle: Contains the ilium, ischium, pubis, and sacrum.

Pathologies of the Skeletal System:

Ankylosing Spondylitis: Progressive **autoimmune** disorder resulting in **degeneration** of **intervertebral discs**. Disc degeneration leads to loss of curvature of the spine, fusion of vertebrae together, and loss of motion at the site of bone fusion.

Baker's Cyst: Formation of a sac **behind the knee** as a result of **synovial fluid** leaking from the joint cavity.

Bursitis: Inflammation of a **bursa sac**, usually due to trauma to a bursa. Often presents with **fluid buildup**, restricting range of motion at the site if around a joint.

Dislocation: Displacement of a bone from its normal location, damaging tissues around the area. Severely weakens the joint following the dislocation, allowing for further dislocation to occur.

Fracture: A **break** in a bone. A **simple** fracture remains **inside** the skin, while a **compound** fracture **breaks through** the skin.

Gout: Excessive **uric acid** buildup in the body, resulting in a severely inflamed **big toe**, and may also be seen in the arms and hands as well. Caused by an inability of the body to eliminate uric acid normally.

Herniated Disc: Protrusion of the gelatinous center of an intervertebral disc, known as the **nucleus pulposus**, through the tough cartilaginous portion of an intervertebral disc, known as the **annulus fibrosis**. Results in compression of spinal nerves, producing pain.

Kyphosis: Hyper-curvature of the **thoracic vertebrae**, producing a hump-back appearance. Also known as **Dowager's Hump**. Can be caused by tight chest muscles, weakened back muscles, or other conditions such as osteoporosis or ankylosing spondylitis.

Lordosis: Hyper-curvature of the **lumbar vertebrae**, forcing the vertebrae anteriorly. Also known as **Swayback**. Can be caused by hypertonicity of the psoas major, or weakness in the rectus abdominis. May also result in overstretching of the hamstrings.

Osteoarthritis: Erosion of the **hyaline cartilage** between articulating bones. Results in increased friction between the bones, causing pain and inflammation. Also known as "wear and tear" arthritis.

Osteomyelitis: Bacterial infection affecting the bone, which may enter into the **marrow** and **periosteum**.

Osteoporosis: Degeneration of bone tissue, due to a lack of **calcium** entering into the bones. Usually seen in **post-menopausal women**, due to a lack of **estrogen** production. Bones become thin and brittle, making them prone to injuries such as fracture.

Rheumatoid Arthritis: Autoimmune disorder in which the body's immune system attacks **synovial membranes** surrounding joints. Upon degeneration, the membrane is replaced by **fibrous tissue**, which restricts range of motion in the joints. Usually takes place at the metacarpophalangeal joints of the hands. The fingers are turned to a medial position, making function difficult.

Scoliosis: Lateral curvature of the vertebrae, most commonly in the thoracic vertebrae. Can be caused by severely hypertonic muscles, congenital deformities of the vertebral column, and poor posture.

Shin Splints: Pain along the **medial anterior shaft of the tibia,** usually due to tearing of muscular attachments. Results from over-training, running or jumping on hard surfaces, wearing the wrong equipment, etc. Also known as medial tibia stress syndrome and periostitis.

Sprain: Injury to a **ligament**, caused by overstretching or tearing of a ligament.

      Grade 1: Stretching of a ligament **without tearing**.

      Grade 2: **Partial tearing** of a ligament that presents with **bruising** and inflammation.

      Grade 3: **Complete rupture** of a ligament which requires surgery to repair.

<u>Urinary System</u>: Consists of the **kidneys, ureters, urinary bladder,** and **urethra**. Responsible for **elimination** of waste from the body, **reabsorption** of nutrients, and **pH regulation**.

Kidneys: Filtrate and **reabsorb** substances back into the body. Regulates the amount of **electrolytes** in the body. Inside each kidney, there are **one million nephrons**, which are responsible for reabsorbing vitamins, electrolytes, and water back into the blood stream.

Ureters: Transport urine from the kidneys to the bladder.

Urinary Bladder: Stores urine.

Urethra: Transports urine from the urinary bladder out of the body.

Pathologies of the Urinary System:

Cystitis: Bacterial infection of the **urinary bladder**, resulting in bloody urine, pain, and increased urination frequency.

Pyelonephritis: Bacterial infection of the **kidneys**, usually results after obtaining cystitis.

Uremia: Excessive amounts of **urea** in the **blood stream**, usually a sign of **renal failure**, caused by inability of the kidneys to filter properly.

Urinary Tract Infection: Bacterial infection typically affecting both the **urethra** and **urinary bladder**.

Vital Signs

Vital Signs: Indication of the body's ability to **maintain homeostasis**. Temperature, pulse, blood pressure, and respiration are the primary vital signs.

Temperature may be measured in several different areas, utilizing a thermometer.

Oral/Sublingual: Thermometer inserted **under the tongue**. Baseline temperature is 98.6 degrees Fahrenheit

Axillary: Thermometer inserted into the **armpit**. Baseline temperature is one degree less than oral/sublingual.

Rectal: Thermometer inserted into the **rectum**. Baseline temperature is one degree higher than oral/sublingual.

Aural: Measures temperature of the tympanic membrane **inside the ear**.

Pulse: Used to determine **heart rhythm** and **heart rate**.

Heart Rhythm: Regularity of **heart beat**.

Heart Rate: Beats **per minute**.

Radial Pulse: Read at the **lateral side** of the wrist, most common site to read pulse.

Ulnar Pulse: Read at the **medial side** of the wrist.

Apical Pulse: Read using a stethoscope at the **apex of the heart**.

Brachial Pulse: Read at the **medial side of arm**, commonly used to determine pulse of infants.

Carotid Pulse: Read at the **neck**, used to determine pulse in adults.

Femoral Pulse: Read at the **proximal anterior thigh**, used to determine pulse in adults.

Popliteal Pulse: Read at the **back of the knee**.

Dorsalis Pedis Pulse: Read on the **dorsal surface** of the foot.

Blood Pressure: Pressure felt in arteries during **normal circulation**.

Systolic Pressure: Pressure felt in arteries as blood **passes through them**(heart beating).

Diastolic Pressure: Pressure felt in arteries when the heart is **relaxed**(not beating).

In a blood pressure reading of 120/80, 120 represents the **Systolic Pressure**, and 80 represents **Diastolic Pressure**.

Respiration: The act of **breathing**. Measured by observing breathing pattern, rate, and depth of breath.

Inspiration: Inhalation of air to bring **oxygen** into the body.

Expiration: Exhalation of air to eliminate **carbon dioxide** and other waste.

Normal Vital Sign Ranges:
Temperature:
     Infant: 96-100
     1-5 years: 98-100
     6-10 years: 97-99.5
     11-15 years: 97.5-100.5
     Adult: 97.5-100.5
Pulse:
     Infant: 80-160 beats per minute
     1-5 years: 75-130 beats per minute
     6-10 years: 70-115 beats per minute
     11-15 years: 55-110 beats per minute
     Adult: 60-100 beats per minute
Blood Pressure:
     Infant: 60-95/50-65
     1-5 years: 80-100/50-70
     6-10 years: 80-120/50-80
     11-15 years: 95-135/58-88
     Adult: 90-120/60-80
Respiration:
     Infant: 25-40 breaths per minute
     1-5 years: 20-30 breaths per minute
     6-10 years: 18-25 breaths per minute
     11-15 years: 16-25 breaths per minute
     Adult: 12-20 breaths per minute

CPR and First Aid

CPR: Cardiopulmonary Resuscitation

First Aid:
Emergency Triage: Classifying injuries by **severity**, **treatment urgency**, and **treatment location**.
Universal Precautions: Treating every person and fluid as **contaminated** or **infectious**. Used to properly contain blood-borne pathogens. Wear **gloves** and other protective equipment, avoiding contact with blood.
Documentation: Taking note of patient **emergencies**.
Good Samaritan Law: Law designed to **protect** person performing first aid or offering care to unresponsive persons **outside** a medical setting.

Heat Injuries:
Heat Exhaustion: High body temperature with **excessive sweating**.
Heat Cramps: Tightening and involuntary spasming of muscles due to **dehydration** and loss of **electrolytes**.
Heat Stroke: High body temperature with **lack** of sweating, due to extreme dehydration.

Cold Injuries:
Hypothermia: Body temperature dropping **below 90** degrees Fahrenheit
Frostbite: Formation of **ice crystals** in soft tissues, resulting in **necrosis** of affected areas.

Burns:
First degree burn: Most common, least serious. Most common form is a sunburn, affecting the **epidermis**, resulting in inflammation and irritation of the skin. Apply cold dressings and cold water to the affected area.
Second degree burn: Burn moves through the **epidermis** into the **dermis**, which leads to the development of **blisters** and swelling. Contact EMS, cover burned areas with sterile bandages.
Third degree burn: Burn moves through the **epidermis** and the **dermis**, into

the **subcutaneous layer**. May also involve muscles, tendons, ligaments, and bones. Results in **necrosis** and scarring of the skin, and may lead to infection if not treated properly. Contact EMS, cover burned areas with sterile bandages.

Rule of 9's: Used to determine extent of **burns** by total body area involved.

Head and Neck: 9%
Right Arm: 9%
Left Arm: 9%
Right Leg: 18%
Left Leg: 18%
Thorax: 18%
Abdomen: 9%
Lower Back: 9%
Groin: 1%

Chemical Burns: Rinse with water, contact EMS.
Thermal Burns: Rinse with water, contact EMS.
Electrical Burns: Contact EMS.

Wounds:
Open Wound: Breaking of skin or membrane which results in exposure of the underlying tissues.
Incision: A clean **cut**.
Laceration: A cut producing **jagged edges**.
Abrasion: Scraped skin. Cleanse with soap and water, apply sterile bandage.
Puncture: Hole resulting from **piercing object**. Allow to bleed for a few minutes, cleanse with soap and water, apply sterile bandage.

Bites and Stings:
Animal Bites: If bite results in **puncture**, try to force bleeding to clear out bacteria. Cleanse with soap and water, apply sterile dressing.
Rabies: Viral infection transferred via saliva.
Insect Sting: Scrape skin with a hard, flat, sharp object such as a knife to remove **stinger**. Cleanse skin with soap and water. If asphyxiation is suspected, contact EMS.
Snake Bite: Notify EMS, immobilize area **below heart**, cleanse area with

soap and water.

Spider Bite: Cleanse bite with soap and water, immobilize area **below heart**. Suggest patient seek medical attention.

Scorpion Stings: Cleanse bite with soap and water, immobilize area **below heart**. Suggest patient seek medical attention.

Orthopedic Injuries:

RICE: Rest, Ice, Compression, Elevation.

Sprain: Injury to a **ligament**, caused by overstretching or tearing of a ligament. Recommend patient utilize RICE in acute stage.

    Grade 1: Stretching of a ligament without tearing.

    Grade 2: Partial tearing of a ligament that presents with bruising and inflammation.

    Grade 3: Complete rupture of a ligament which requires surgery to repair.

Strain: An injury to a **muscle or tendon**, may be caused by overexertion or overstretching. Recommend patient utilize RICE in acute stage.

Fracture: A **break** in a bone. A **simple** fracture remains **inside the skin**, while a **compound** fracture breaks **through the skin**. Immobilize area using splint.

Poisoning:

Inhalation: Introduced to the body via **breathing**. Examples include carbon monoxide or carbon dioxide. Patients might be given antidote, and require breathing support via oxygen mask.

Injection: Introducing harmful substance into the body via **insect stings**, **needles, sharp objects**, or **bites**. Usually requires use of antidote to combat poison.

Absorption: Introduced into the body via skin **absorption**. Examples include **insecticides**. Area should be cleaned thoroughly with water.

Ingestion: Introducing harmful substances via **swallowing**. Depending on substance, patient may require induced vomiting or drinking milk or water.

Instruments

Percussion Hammer: Used to test **reflexes**, may also be known as a **reflex hammer**.

Tuning Fork: Tests **hearing**.

Nasal Speculum: Instrument inserted into the **nostrils** that open the nasal passages, allowing for further visual inspection.

Otoscope: Allows visual inspection of the **tympanic membrane** inside the ear.

Audioscope: Used to test the loss of **hearing**.

Ophthalmoscope: Examine the **inner portions** of the **eyes**.

Stethoscope: Used to listen to various **sounds** throughout the body, such as **heart beat**, **lung function** and **blood pressure**.

Laryngoscope: Used to examine the **larynx**.

Vaginal Speculum: Instrument inserted into the **vaginal canal** that opens the vagina. Used primarily during **pap smears** and examination of the pelvis.

Anoscope: Used to examine the **rectum and large intestine**.

Proctoscope: Used to examine the **rectum and large intestine**.

Sigmoidscope: Used to examine the last portion of the **large intestine**.

Autoclave: Used to **sterilize** instruments. **Outer** chamber increases **pressure**, **inner** chamber **sterilizes**. Uses steam above **250 degrees Fahrenheit**

Forceps: Used to **pull**, **grasp**, or **handle** tissue or equipment.

Scissors: Used to **cut** bandages, **sutures**, and **tissues**.

Scalpel: Small **knife** used to perform **incisions** or **excise** tissue from the body.

Retractor: Holds layers of tissue **open** to allow tissues underneath to be accessed.

Sutures: Used to **close wounds**.

Skin Staples: Type of **suture** used that must be removed when the would has **healed** completely.

Dressings: Used on **wounds** to prevent further introduction of microorganisms. Secured to the body using **bandages**.

Nebulizer: Delivers medication in **vapor** form via inhalation.

Electrocardiograph: Also called **EKG** or **ECG**, measures the cycle of **electric currents** passing through the heart.

12-Lead Electrocardiograph: Uses **twelve leads** to record **electrical current** information. Consists of **limb leads**, **augmented limb leads**, and **chest leads**.

Single-Channel Electrocardiograph: Uses **one lead** to record information.

Microscope: Used to view objects **not visible** to the naked eye.

Catheter: Tube inserted into the **urinary bladder**.

Centrifuge: Device used to separate **solids** from **liquids**.

Hemocytometer: Microscope used to count **blood cells**, **thrombocytes**, etc. Most common type is **Neubauer**.

Urinometer: Measures the specific **gravity** of **urine**.

Refractometer: Measures **refraction** of **light** through a **liquid**.

Spirometer: Measures **volume** of air intake and output.

Sphygmomanometer: Measures **blood pressure**.

EKG/ECG:

P Wave: Represents **depolarization** of the **right atrium** and **left atrium**, visualization of firing of the **SA node**.

PR Interval: Time it takes for a **nerve impulse** to travel from the **SA node** through the **atria** into the **ventricles**.

QRS Complex: Represents the **conduction** of an electrical impulse from the **bundle of His** through the **ventricles**.

ST Segment: Represents **depolarization** of the **right ventricle** and **left ventricle**.

T Wave: Represents **repolarization** of the **right ventricle** and **left ventricle**.

Artifacts: Abnormalities in an EKG reading caused by **non-cardiac origins**.

Intentional Artifacts: May be caused by **pacemakers**.

Medications and Injections

Local Anesthetics: Used to **numb** an area which **reduces pain**. Commonly **lidocaine** is used. Administered via **needle injection**.

Analgesics: Pain relievers.

Antacids: Reduces activity of **acids** in the stomach.

Antibiotics: Combats **microorganism** growth, specifically **bacterium**.

Anticoagulants: Reduces formation of **blood clots**.

Antifungals: Destroy **fungus**.

Antihistamines: Reduces effects of **histamines** on the body.

Anti-inflammatory Agents: Reduce **inflammation**.

Antipyretics: Reduce **body temperature**.

Antivirals: Combat **virus** reproduction.

Broncho-dilators: Dilate **bronchial tubes**.

Decongestants: Reduce **inflammation** in **nasal cavity**.

Diuretics: Increases **urine** production by **kidneys**.

Insulin: Helps control **diabetes**.

Sedatives: Relax and **calm** the body.

Ampule: Small **glass** container, broken at the neck to access medication.

Vial: Glass or plastic container sealed by a **rubber stopper** at the top.

Needles: Used to administer **injections**.

Gauge: Diameter of a needle. The **higher** the number gauge, the **smaller** the needle diameter. The **lower** the number gauge, the **larger** the needle diameter.

Types of Injections:

Intradermal: Injection into the **dermis** at a **10** degree to **15** degree angle.

Subcutaneous: Injection into the **subcutaneous layer of the skin** at a **45** degree angle.

Intramuscular: Injection **into the muscle** at a **90** degree angle.

Common Injection Sites:

Intradermal: Anterior **forearm**, posterior **arm**, **thorax**, **scapular** region.

Intramuscular: Deltoid, vastus lateralis, ventrogluteal, dorsogluteal.

Subcutaneous: Posterior and lateral **arm**, abdomen around the **umbilicus**, anterior **thigh**.

Nutrition

Seven Nutrients: Proteins, carbohydrates, fats, minerals, vitamins, fiber, water.

ADA recommends 65% **carbohydrates**, 25% **fats**, 15% **protein**.

Vitamin A: Most common type is **beta-carotene**, found in orange and yellow fruits and vegetables. Maintains healthy **skin**, **mucous** membranes, **bones**, and **teeth**.

Vitamin K: Blood **clotting**.

Vitamin D: Produced in the **skin** when exposed to the sun, also fortified in many foods. Allows the body to absorb **calcium**.

Vitamin E: Found in vegetable oils, nuts, leafy vegetables. Helps to protect tissue from **free radicals**, assists in the formation of **erythrocytes**.

Vitamin C: Found in citrus fruits and melons, assists in the body's **immunity** and protection of tissue from **free radicals**.

Vitamin B6: Assists in the production of **hemoglobin** and **antibodies**. Deficiency can result in **anemia**.

Vitamin B12: Assists in formation of **erythrocytes**. Deficiency can result in **pernicious anemia**.

Potassium: Helps with **muscle contraction** and synthesizing **protein**.

Calcium: Most **abundant** mineral in the body. Provides **strong bones**, allows **muscle contraction**.

Iron: Hemoglobin for oxygen and carbon dioxide transport.

Sodium: Maintains **pH** balance, helps transport **nerve impulses**.

Magnesium: Maintains **strong bones**, regulates **heartbeat**.

Letterhead: Business stationary. Lists name, address, phone, usually at top of paper. 8.5" x 11" is standard. 8.5" x 14" is legal.

Envelopes: A number **10** envelope is known as "business size", measures 4 1/8" x 9 1/2". Invoices and statements use envelopes sized between number 6, measuring 3 5/8" x 6 1/2", and number 10. Contains transparent windows to show address.

Pre-addressed Envelopes: Used to **return** payments to office.

Tan Kraft: Clasp envelopes, used for large documents.

Padded Envelopes: Used to send objects which may be otherwise **damaged** in transit.

Parts of a Business Letter:

Margin: Area around **edges** of a form, blank. **One inch** is standard.

Letterhead: Lists name, address, and phone number, usually at the **top** of the paper.

Dateline: Contains month, day, year. Begins **three** lines below letterhead, on **Line 15**. The month is always **spelled out**, with a **comma** after the day.

Inside Address: Name and address of the person receiving the letter.

Key: Typing the address on the **left** margin, **2-4** spaces down from the date, **2-4** lines in length. Use a Courtesy Title, including the **full name**. Numbers 1-9 are **spelled out**, and anything over 10 is typed in **numerals**. Spell out "Street", "Drive", etc. Use the **full city name** with the **two letter state abbreviation**. **One** space after state abbreviation, add **zip code**.

Attention Line: Used to send a letter to a **specific person** in a company.

Salutation: "**Dear** _____", followed by a colon.

Subject Line: Allows the reader to understand the subject of the letter. Placed on the second line **below** the salutation.

Body: Two lines below the salutation or subject.

Complimentary Closing: Placed two lines **below** the body. Example is "Sincerely".

Signature Block: First line is the **name** of the letter writer. Business title is placed on the **second line**. Align with the **complimentary closing**, four lines below.

Identification Line: Writer's **initials**. Typed on the **left**, two lines **below** the signature block.

Notations: Number of enclosures included, **names** of others receiving a copy of the letter. Notations are placed on the **left side**, one or two lines **below** the Identification Line.

Punctuation:

Open Punctuation: Uses **no punctuation** with Attention, Salutation, Complimentary Closing, Signature Block, Enclosure, and Copy Notifications.

Mixed Punctuation: Uses a **colon** after Attention and Salutation, a **comma** after the Complimentary Closing, a **colon** or **period** after the Enclosure Notation, and a **colon** after the Copy Notation.

Letter Styles:

Full-Block Style: All lines flush **left**.

Modified Block Style: Dateline, Complimentary Closing, Signature Block, and Notations aligned at the **center** of the page.

Simplified Style: No Salutation, Subject placed **between** the Address and Body, all text to the **left**, **no** Complimentary Closing, sender's name and title in **caps** on a single line at the **end** of the letter.

Address Placement: Address is bordered by a **one inch** margin on the left and right, **5/8"** margin on the bottom. The top of the city/state/zip code line should be no higher than **2 1/4"** from the bottom.

Address Format: Type the address using **single space lines** and **block format**. The first line is the **name**. The last line is the **city/state/zip code**.

State Abbreviations:

Alabama: AL	Montana: MT
Alaska: AK	Nebraska: NE
Arizona: AZ	Nevada: NV
Arkansas: AR	New Hampshire: NH
California: CA	New Jersey: NJ
Colorado: CO	New Mexico: NM
Connecticut: CT	New York: NY
Delaware: DE	North Carolina: NC
Florida: FL	North Dakota: ND
Georgia: GA	Ohio: OH
Hawaii: HI	Oklahoma: OK
Idaho: ID	Oregon: OR
Illinois: IL	Pennsylvania: PA
Indiana: IN	Rhode Island: RI
Iowa: IA	South Carolina: SC
Kansas: KS	South Dakota: SD
Kentucky: KY	Tennessee: TN
Louisiana: LA	Texas: TX
Maine: ME	Utah: UT
Maryland: MD	Vermont: VT
Massachusetts: MA	Virginia: VA
Michigan: MI	Washington: WA
Minnesota: MN	Washington DC: DC
Mississippi: MS	West Virginia: WV
Missouri: MO	Wisconsin: WI
	Wyoming: WY

Financial Management

Omnibus Budget Reconciliation Act: Requires **physical reimbursement** for Medicare based on a fee schedule.

Geographical Practice Cost Index: Adjusts **physician fees**.

National Conversion Factor: Determines **fee schedules** for all health care services.

Credit: Debt **borrowed** to be paid by debtor at a later date.

Accounts Receivable: Money owed to the office.

Collection: Acquiring **funds** or **payment** owed to the office.

Bankruptcy: Liquidation of **assets** to repay debts.

Chapter 7 Bankruptcy: Assets are **sold off** and funds distributed to creditors.

Chapter 13 Bankruptcy: Provides **protection** to debtors who are in the process of arranging payments over three or five years.

Patient Billing Statement: Mailed once a month detailing **balances due**.

Collection Agency: Company used in order to collect **outstanding debts**.

Fair Debt Collection Act: Prevents **unfair** or **abusive** collection practices.

Legal Knowledge

HIPAA: Health Insurance Accountability Act of 1996. Enacted August 21, 1996. Created by US Department of Heath and Human Services.

Title I: Health Care Portability. Allows persons to carry health insurance from **one job** to **another job**.

Title II: Prevention of Heath Care Fraud and Abuse, Administrative Simplification, and Medical Liability Reform.

Privacy Rule: Protects all individually **identifiable** health information. Assures health information of individuals is **protected** while allowing health information to be **transferred** between healthcare providers to provide high-quality health care.

> Individual's past, present, future physical or mental health or condition. Provision of health care to individual.
>
> Past, present, or future payment for provision of health care to individual.

Permitted Uses and Disclosures:

> To the individual.
>
> Treatment, Payment, Health Care Operations.
>
> Uses and Disclosures with Opportunity to Agree or Object
>
> Incidental Use and Disclosure.
>
> Public Interest and Benefit Activities.
>
> Limited Data Set.

Security Rule: Specifies **protection** of patient **information** via computers and internet.

Title VII of the Civil Rights Act of 1964: Prevents **discrimination** in the workplace or place of business.

Consent: Patient giving **permission** for examination, treatment, or diagnoses.

Informed Consent: Right of patient to **understand** and **receive** all information related to their condition and treatment options.

Liability: Being **legally responsible** for every aspect of a medical practice.

Malpractice: Error in diagnosis or treatment.

Negligence: Failure of a medical professional to perform **essential actions** that result in **harm** to a patient.

Confidentiality: Keeping patient information **private and protected** at all times.

Code of Ethics: Guiding **moral principles** of right and wrong.

Types of Medical Businesses:

Sole Proprietorship: Medical practice owned by **one person**.

Partnership: Medical practices owned by **two or more** persons.

Group Practice: Three or more physicians sharing income and expenses.

Professional Corporations: Authorized by state to act as a **single entity**.

Communication:

Body Language: Non-verbal communication. Types include touch, eye contact, facial expressions, and posture.

Active Listening: Listening to the patient and **replying** to statements being made.

Passive Listening: Listening to the patient **without** offering a reply.

Open Ended Question: Questions used when asking for **feedback** from patients.

Close Ended Question: Questions used that require only a **yes or no** response.

Health Insurance

Group Health Benefits: Benefits offered by **employers**, **associations**, **unions**, or other **organizations**.

Dependent: Spouse or **child** covered by one person's insurance policy.

Deductible: Amount required to be paid by the **policy-holder** before insurance payments begin.

Medicare: Provides health insurance to the **elderly**, sponsored by the government.

Medicare Part A: Covers **hospital** expenses.

Medicare Part B: Covers physician **fees**, **immunizations**, **screening** tests, and **diagnostic** tests.

Medicaid: Provides health insurance to **low-income persons**. Regulated by both state and federal governments.

TRICARE: Provides health insurance for dependents of **active** military personnel, **retired** military personnel, and dependents of **deceased** military personnel.

HMO: Network of health care providers who have contracted with the health insurer.

PPO: Preferred Provider Organization. List of providers **contracted** to health care plans.

Coding

ICD-9-CM: DX coding system used to code **morbidity**.

E Codes: Used for classifying cause of **injury, poisoning,** or adverse **drug** reactions.

M Codes: Used by **tumor** registries to identify **tumors** and **growths**.

V Codes: Used to describe circumstances other than **disease** or **injury**. Examples include preventative care, chemotherapy, or radiation therapy.

CMS-1500: Used to document up to **four** different conditions.

CPT: Coding system used to document **procedures**. CPT manual contains **six** sections.

Assignments

The following are assignments you should complete to further test your knowledge. There are crossword puzzles, word searches, matching, and labeling assignments. Have fun with these! The hard part is coming up afterwards!

While filling these out, do them all from memory, not by looking back at your previously filled-out study guide. This is yet another way to make sure you know the information. Only look back at your study guide if you absolutely positively can't remember the information.

Body Systems
Complete the crossword below

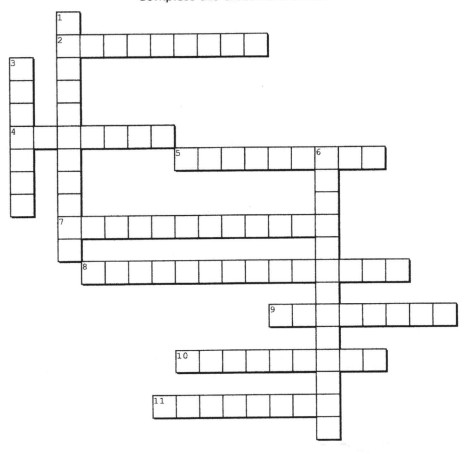

Across

2. Produces hormones, consists of glands
4. Sensory reception and evaluation, consists of brain and spinal cord
5. Breaks down food and absorbs nutrients, consists of the alimentary canal
7. Allows for reproduction, consists of genitalia
8. Pumps blood, consists of heart and blood vessels
9. Protects the body and provides support, consists of bones
10. Aids in defense against pathogens, consists of lymph nodes and lymph
11. Creates heat and movement, consists of muscles

Down

1. Circulates air in and out of the lungs, consists of the lungs and airways
3. Filters, reabsorbs, and eliminates substances, consists of the kidneys and bladder
6. Protects the body, consists of skin, hair, nails, and sweat glands

Medical Instruments

Complete the crossword below

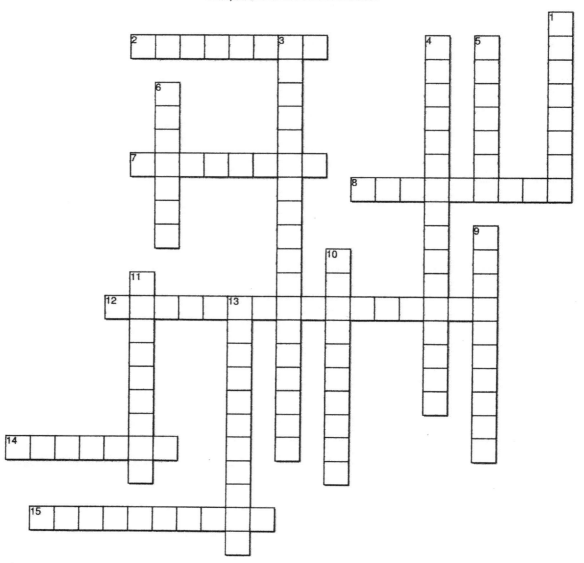

Across
2. Used to drain the urinary bladder
7. Used to cut bandages, tissues, or sutures
8. Used to sterilize instruments using steam
12. Used to test reflexes
14. Used to close wounds
15. Used to examine objects not visible to the naked eye

Down
1. Used to examine inner ear
3. Used to measure electric currents through the heart
4. Used to measure blood pressure
5. Small knife used to make incisions
6. Used to grasp tissue or instruments
9. Used to hold tissues open
10. Used to separate solids from liquids
11. Used to deliver medication in vapor form
13. Used to listen to sounds in the body

Business Letters

Complete the crossword below

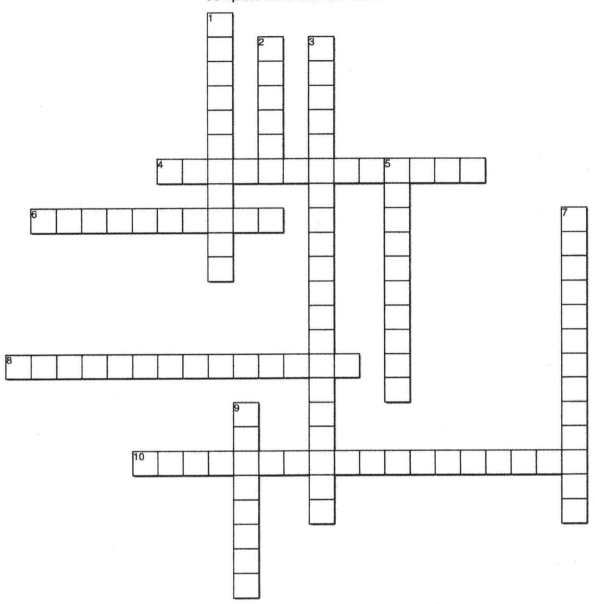

Across

4. Used to send letter to a specific person in a company

6. 'Dear _____'

8. Name of letter writer, comes after 'Sincerely'

10. Writer's initials

Down

1. Tells reader what the topic of the letter is

2. Area around the edges of a form

3. 'Sincerely', closing of a letter

5. Lists name, address, and phone number of business

7. Name of person receiving letter

9. Contains month, day, and year

Medications

Find the medications based on what they're used for!

```
W  J  A  P  K  D  H  D  W  E  A  N  T  I  F  U  N  G  A  L
V  S  M  C  I  Q  T  N  J  Q  W  W  B  Y  E  Y  X  F  J  X
C  B  L  X  A  E  N  I  M  A  T  S  I  H  I  T  N  A  U  N
M  I  A  Z  N  A  N  T  I  B  I  O  T  I  C  L  H  S  B  Q
N  A  Q  W  T  K  T  F  U  K  C  D  L  O  L  B  V  R  R  G
A  N  T  I  I  N  F  L  A  M  M  A  T  O  R  Y  O  P  X  Z
T  D  R  U  V  Z  U  J  Z  S  L  H  C  G  O  N  A  B  V  J
H  B  Q  E  I  I  N  M  X  J  R  A  H  X  C  N  E  L  W  O
P  Y  R  F  R  U  N  Z  I  C  L  F  O  H  T  K  V  V  X  E
B  R  M  B  A  I  N  B  V  A  U  G  O  I  N  I  I  O  D  X
P  Y  A  I  L  S  D  X  N  I  T  D  P  P  A  M  T  N  W  C
K  A  Z  U  G  Y  S  E  A  F  I  Y  Z  S  T  X  A  Z  R  X
B  G  S  X  Z  F  S  N  D  L  R  J  R  G  S  V  D  S  Z  N
S  N  J  X  U  T  T  N  A  E  B  T  P  G  E  D  E  G  I  W
I  Z  Y  B  H  A  N  T  T  T  A  N  A  L  G  E  S  I  C  P
O  S  Q  E  C  A  O  I  F  T  K  P  I  P  N  U  E  N  J  O
G  T  T  I  R  R  C  I  S  V  Z  I  Z  L  O  M  M  B  H  S
E  I  D  J  S  N  G  K  W  S  L  K  W  U  C  C  B  Y  A  Y
C  T  N  A  L  U  G  A  O  C  I  T  N  A  E  H  G  S  M  J
C  I  T  E  R  U  I  D  E  F  L  B  Y  R  D  V  I  K  O  M
```

Numbs a localized area	Pain reliever	Reduces activity of acid in stomach
Combats growth of bacteria	Prevents blood clots	Destroys fungus
Reduces effects of histamines on the body	Reduces inflammation	Reduces fever
Combats virus reproduction	Dilates bronchial tubes	Reduces inflammation in the nasal cavity
Increases production of urine	Helps control diabetes	Calms and relaxes the body

Word Roots

Write the letter of the correct match next to each problem.

1. _____ Necr/o		a. Muscle
2. _____ Leuk/o		b. Liver
3. _____ Melan/o		c. Fat
4. _____ Cost/o		d. Kidney
5. _____ Spondyl/o		e. Arm
6. _____ Gastr/o		f. Blood
7. _____ Derm/o		g. Black
8. _____ Chondr/o		h. Tongue
9. _____ Adip/o		i. Brain
10. _____ Hepat/o		j. Rib
11. _____ Gloss/o		k. Spine
12. _____ My/o		l. Stomach
13. _____ Nephr/o		m. White
14. _____ Brachi/o		n. Vein
15. _____ Cardi/o		o. Lung
16. _____ Erythr/o		p. Skin
17. _____ Encephal/o		q. Cartilage
18. _____ Hem/o		r. Death
19. _____ Pneum/o		s. Red
20. _____ Phleb/o		t. Heart

Prefixes

Write the letter of the correct match next to each problem.

1.	_____	auto-	a.	Together
2.	_____	a-	b.	Change
3.	_____	hyper-	c.	Without
4.	_____	meta-	d.	Two
5.	_____	mal-	e.	Against
6.	_____	syn-	f.	Above
7.	_____	homeo-	g.	Through
8.	_____	hypo-	h.	Equal
9.	_____	inter-	i.	Slow
10.	_____	dia-	j.	Same
11.	_____	bi-	k.	Large
12.	_____	macro-	l.	Towards
13.	_____	brady-	m.	Small
14.	_____	micro-	n.	Around
15.	_____	anti-	o.	Bad
16.	_____	iso-	p.	Excessive
17.	_____	circum-	q.	Inside
18.	_____	endo-	r.	Below
19.	_____	af-	s.	Self
20.	_____	epi-	t.	Between

Suffixes
Write the letter of the correct match next to each problem.

1. _____	-ectomy	a.	Nourishment
2. _____	-blast	b.	Blood
3. _____	-pnea	c.	Production
4. _____	-crine	d.	Swelling
5. _____	-cision	e.	Resembling
6. _____	-trophy	f.	Condition
7. _____	-algia	g.	Skin
8. _____	-stasis	h.	Standing still
9. _____	-emia	i.	Paralysis
10. _____	-derma	j.	Break
11. _____	-plegia	k.	Protein
12. _____	-gen	l.	Germ cell
13. _____	-phagia	m.	Removal
14. _____	-globin	n.	Dissolve
15. _____	-clast	o.	Cutting
16. _____	-edema	p.	Pain
17. _____	-osis	q.	Eating
18. _____	-cyte	r.	Breathing
19. _____	-oid	s.	Secrete
20. _____	-lysis	t.	Cell

Name This Instrument

_____

Name This Instrument

_____

Name This Instrument

_____

Name This Instrument

_____

Name This Instrument

_____

Name This Instrument

_____

Name This Instrument

_____

Name This Instrument

_____

Name This Instrument

Name This Bone

_____

Name This Bone

_____

Name This Bone

_____

Name This Bone

_____

Name This Bone

_____

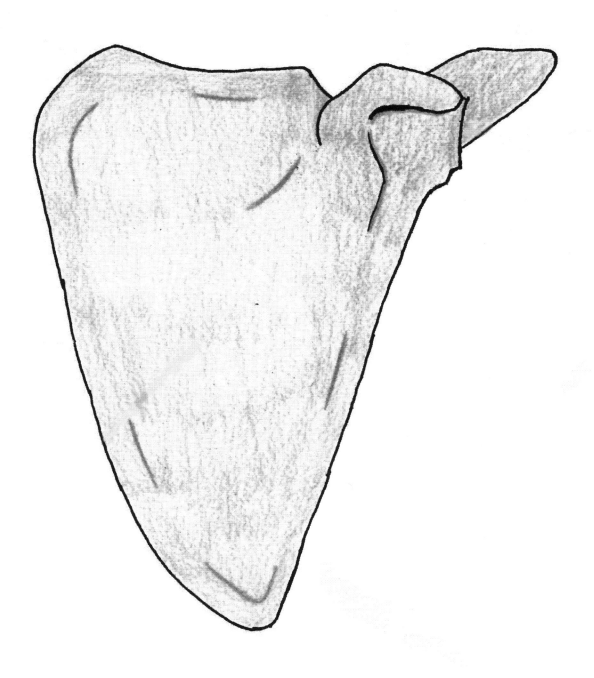

Name This Bone

_____

Name This Bone

_____

Practice Tests

When taking your practice tests, make sure you are utilizing many of the test taking techniques discussed earlier in the book. What I always recommend is, when taking these tests or any test, if you are given a piece of scratch paper, write down as many of the test-taking techniques as you can remember. This way, if you start feeling nervous or anxious about a specific question, or if you just don't know the answer, you can look back at the techniques, and it could help you figure out the answer!

These tests are 200 questions each, covering a wide range of topics. Make sure you don't go back and look in the book for the answers. Being able to come up with the answer in your head is paramount. Remember, you won't have your book with you when you take your test, so don't fall back on it when you don't know an answer.

I recommend writing your answers to these tests on a separate piece of paper. This allows you to take the tests multiple times, and really hone your test-taking techniques.

Good luck on your tests! Remember, your technique in taking your tests can be the difference between passing and failing, so make sure you're doing everything you can do develop these techniques as best you can. I believe in you!

1. CMS-1500 is used to
A. Document procedures
B. Identify tumors
C. Classify cause of injury
D. Document up to four different conditions

2. Primary function of a gland
A. Secretion
B. Protection
C. Absorption
D. Contraction

3. Branching muscle tissue is also called
A. Smooth
B. Skeletal
C. Cardiac
D. Striated

4. The leading cause of lung, oral, and esophageal cancer
A. Industrial dust
B. Cigarette smoking
C. Asbestos
D. Cystic fibrosis

5. Decrease in oxygen traveling throughout the body
A. Hypoplasia
B. Hypoglycemia
C. Hypoxia
D. Hyperplasia

6. The Omnibus Budget Reconciliation Act
A. Requires physical reimbursement for Medicare based on a fee schedule
B. Adjusts physician fees
C. Liquidates assets to repay debts
D. Determines fee schedules for all health care services

7. Blood pressure is measured using which of the following instruments
A. Spirometer
B. Hemocytometer
C. Sphygmomanometer
D. Electrocardiograph

8. Depolarization of the right atrium and left atrium in an EKG is represented by
A. PR Interval
B. QRS Complex
C. P Wave
D. ST Segment

9. Universal precautions are
A. Considering every fluid and person as contaminated or infectious
B. Noting all emergencies involving patients
C. Classifying an injury based on urgency, location, and severity
D. Protecting a person performing first aid from potential lawsuits

10. The pulmonary arteries carry blood from the right ventricle to
A. Left atrium
B. Rest of the body
C. Aorta
D. Lungs

11. Nausea, vomiting, and fatigue with yellowing of the skin may be the result of
A. Hepatitis
B. Food poisoning
C. Diarrhea
D. Meningitis

12. T lymphocytes are produced by which gland
A. Thymus
B. Thalamus
C. Pituitary
D. Pineal

13. PPE is known as
A. Professional priorities in emergencies
B. Personal protective equipment
C. People profiting from the environment
D. Pulse performed in the ear

14. Ischemia may ultimately result in
A. Phlebitis
B. Arteriosclerosis
C. Necrosis
D. Varicose veins

15. Classifying an injury by severity, urgency, and location is known as
A. Universal precautions
B. Emergency triage
C. Documentation
D. Sterilization

16. Breaking the skin resulting in exposure of underlying tissue
A. Incision
B. Laceration
C. Abrasion
D. Open wound

17. A sedative has what affect on the body
A. Increases urine production
B. Relaxes and calms
C. Reduces body temperature
D. Reduces inflammation

18. The area around the edges of a form is called
A. Dateline
B. Inside Address
C. Margin
D. Letterhead

19. Due to having a shorter urethra, women are more prone to developing the following condition than men
A. Prostatitis
B. Nephritis
C. Cystitis
D. Cholecystitis

20. A blood pressure reading of 140/90 results in a person being diagnosed with
A. Hypertension
B. Hypotension
C. Hyperemia
D. Myocardial infarction

21. The dateline begins how many lines below the letterhead
A. Three lines
B. Five lines
C. Four lines
D. Seven lines

22. Another name for a leukocyte is
A. Thrombocyte
B. Red blood cell
C. Platelet
D. White blood cell

23. Type of envelope used for objects that may be damaged while in transit
A. Tan Kraft
B. Clasp
C. Pre-addressed
D. Padded

24. Instrument used to sterilize medial instruments
A. Retractor
B. Nebulizer
C. Autoclave
D. Centrifuge

25. Temperature reading taken in the ear
A. Sublingual
B. Aural
C. Axillary
D. Oral

26. The functional unit of tissue is called
A. Cell
B. Nerve
C. Blood
D. Muscle

27. Meningitis
A. Inflammation of the meninges, resulting in pressure being placed on the brain
B. Inflammation of the brain, causing increased pressure placed on the cranium
C. Degeneration of brain tissue, resulting in loss of memory
D. Paralysis of one side of the body due to infection of the Herpes Simplex virus

28. Breathing is also known as
A. Respiration
B. Systolic pressure
C. Heart rhythm
D. Blood pressure

29. Vital signs are read using all of the following except
A. Pupil constriction
B. Blood pressure
C. Temperature
D. Respiration

30. The Inside Address contains
A. Month, day, and year
B. Name and address of person receiving letter
C. Name, address, and phone number of the business
D. Subject of the letter

31. TRICARE provides health care to
A. Dependents of active military personnel
B. Elderly
C. Low-income persons
D. High-income persons

32. Coding system used to code morbidity
A. CPT
B. ICD-9-CM
C. E Codes
D. V Codes

33. Repolarization of the right ventricle and left ventricle
A. ST Segment
B. QRS Complex
C. T Wave
D. PR Interval

34. Medication used to numb a localized area
A. Antacid
B. Local anesthetic
C. Antihistamine
D. Insulin

35. An ampule is
A. A small glass container
B. A type of tumor
C. A type of needle
D. A diabetic medication

36. An intradermal injection should enter the dermis at what angle
A. 15 degree
B. 20 degree
C. 45 degree
D. 90 degree

37. Part of a letter that contains the month, day, and year
A. Dateline
B. Letterhead
C. Margin
D. Inside Address

38. All of the following carry blood away from the heart except
A. Capillaries
B. Arteries
C. Arterioles
D. Veins

39. Dopamine is an example of a
A. Neurotransmitter
B. Synapse
C. Neuron
D. Dendrite

40. Money owed to the office is known as
A. Credit
B. Collection
C. Accounts receivable
D. Chapter 7 Bankruptcy

41. Title VII of the Civil Rights Act is designed to
A. Prevent confidential information from being breached
B. Prevent discrimination
C. Protect doctors from lawsuits
D. Give patients the right of informed consent

42. Indentification of tumors and growths is coded using
A. V Codes
B. E Codes
C. CMS-1500
D. M Codes

43. An ST Segment is
A. Depolarization of the right ventricle and left ventricle
B. Repolarization of the right ventricle and left ventricle
C. Time it takes for a nerve impulse to travel from the SA node through the atria into the ventricles
D. Depolarization of the right atrium and left atrium

44. Gravity of urine is measured using a
A. Refractometer
B. Sphygmomanometer
C. Spirometer
D. Urinometer

45. Which of the following is not a structure in the digestive system
A. Gallbladder
B. Spleen
C. Liver
D. Pancreas

46. The trachea lies directly inferior to the
A. Lungs
B. Pharynx
C. Bronchus
D. Larynx

47. Pepsin is located in the
A. Stomach
B. Small intestine
C. Pancreas
D. Gallbladder

48. Volume of intake and output of air is measured by
A. A spirometer
B. A centrifuge
C. A refractometer
D. An otoscope

49. A P Wave represents
A. Depolarization of the right atrium and left atrium
B. Time taken for an impulse to travel from the SA node through the atria into ventricles
C. Depolarization of the right ventricle and left ventricle
D. Conduction of electrical impulse from bundle of His through ventricles

50. Analgesics help relieve
A. Inflammation
B. Congestion
C. Pain
D. Virus reproduction

51. Paralysis of the lower limbs
A. Quadriplegia
B. Hemiplegia
C. Paraplegia
D. Triplegia

52. Genetic disorder leading to muscular degeneration and atrophy
A. Multiple sclerosis
B. Strain
C. Muscular dystrophy
D. Fibromyalgia

53. Bone found in the region of the forearm
A. Radius
B. Humerus
C. Fibula
D. Hamate

54. The gauge of a needle is its
A. Length
B. Width
C. Diameter
D. Sharpness

55. A microscope allows a person to
A. View objects visible to the naked eye
B. View objects not visible to the naked eye
C. View objects that are inside the body
D. View objects that are being electrically stimulated

56. A hemocytometer is used to count
A. Blood cells and thrombocytes
B. Levels of urine in the blood
C. Amount of acidity or alkalinity in a substance
D. Heart beats per minute

57. A thrombus is also known as
A. Aneurysm
B. Embolus
C. Blood clot
D. Platelet

58. An abnormality in an EKG reading that is caused by non-cardiac origins
A. Articulation
B. Arrythmia
C. Artifact
D. Atrial Fibrillation

59. The most common form of local anesthetic is
A. Lidocaine
B. Aspirin
C. Insulin
D. Glucose

60. Conduction of electrical impulse from bundle of His through ventricles
A. P Wave
B. PR Interval
C. T Wave
D. QRS Complex

61. Type of envelope used for return payments to an office
A. Tan Kraft
B. Pre-addressed
C. Inside Address
D. Padded

62. A patient giving permission for examination, treatment, or diagnoses is known as
A. Conformity
B. Liability
C. Consent
D. Confidentiality

63. Active listening is
A. Listening to the patient and replying to statements being made
B. Listening to the patient without offering a reply
C. Questions used when asking for feedback
D. Questions that require only a yes or no response

64. CPT is used to
A. Document procedures
B. Identify tumors and growths
C. Document up to four different conditions
D. Describe circumstances other than disease

65. Cramping and abdominal pain, associated with rectal bleeding, may be a sign of
A. Hiatal hernia
B. Crohn's disease
C. Diverticulosis
D. Ulcerative colitis

66. V Codes are used to
A. Document procedures
B. Document up to four different conditions
C. Describe circumstances other than disease or injury
D. Identify tumors and growths

67. Water is absorbed by the
A. Large intestine
B. Stomach
C. Esophagus
D. Liver

68. Vitamin K contributes to
A. Blood clotting
B. Absorption of calcium
C. Production of hemoglobin
D. Production of erythrocytes

69. The time it takes for nerve impulses to travel from the SA node through the atria into ventricles
A. PR Interval
B. QRS Complex
C. T Wave
D. ST Segment

70. Inspection of the inner portions of the eyes is performed using which instrument
A. Proctoscope
B. Otoscope
C. Stethoscope
D. Ophthalmoscope

71. Temperature reading taken in the armpit
A. Aural
B. Oral
C. Axillary
D. Rectal

72. A laceration is a cut that produces
A. Jagged edges
B. Scraping of skin
C. Clean cut
D. A hole

73. Three or more physicians sharing income and expenses
A. Sole Proprietorship
B. Partnership
C. Professional Corporation
D. Group Practice

74. Non-verbal communication is known as
A. Listening
B. Body Language
C. Active Talking
D. Inactive Talking

75. Coronary arteries
A. Supply blood to the abdomen
B. Supply blood to the head and neck
C. Supply blood to the myocardium
D. Supply blood to the arm and forearm

76. Bronchial tubes branch out into smaller tubes called
A. Larynx
B. Alveoli
C. Trachea
D. Bronchioles

77. Classification causes of injury, poisoning, or adverse reaction to drugs is coded using
A. E Codes
B. M Codes
C. V Codes
D. CPT

78. Injection that enters into the muscle
A. Intradermal
B. Subcutaneous
C. Submuscular
D. Intramuscular

79. The most abundant mineral in the body is
A. Sodium
B. Magnesium
C. Potassium
D. Calcium

80. A number 10 envelope is known as
A. Letterhead
B. Business size
C. Pre-addressed
D. Tan Kraft

81. "Sincerely" is an example of
A. Subject
B. Signature
C. Complimentary Closing
D. Notation

82. Intentional artifacts may be caused by
A. Beta-Blockers
B. Pacemakers
C. Nebulizers
D. Blood thinners

83. Antipyretics are used to
A. Dilate bronchial tubes
B. Reduce inflammation
C. Reduce body temperature
D. Relieve pain

84. Blood passes from the right atrium through the tricuspid valve into the
A. Left ventricle
B. Left atrium
C. Right ventricle
D. Pulmonary artery

85. The study of tumors
A. Pathology
B. Etiology
C. Cardiology
D. Oncology

86. Degeneration of myelin sheaths in the central nervous system
A. Multiple sclerosis
B. Myasthenia gravis
C. Parkinson's disease
D. Alzheimer's disease

87. Instrument used to administer injections
A. Ampule
B. Forceps
C. Needle
D. Vial

88. Vitamin D allows the body to absorb
A. Sodium
B. Beta-carotene
C. Potassium
D. Calcium

89. A pre-addressed envelope is used for
A. Return payments
B. Sending objects that may be damaged
C. Large documents, sealed with clasps
D. Bulk items

90. The dateline begins on which line
A. Line 10
B. Line 7
C. Line 15
D. Line 20

91. The auricle, external acoustic meatus, and tympanic membrane are all parts of the
A. Ear
B. Eye
C. Esophagus
D. Small intestine

92. Valve found between the left atrium and left ventricle
A. Pulmonary
B. Tricuspid
C. Aortic
D. Bicuspid

93. The deltoid is a common injection site for which type of injection
A. Subcutaneous
B. Intradermal
C. Intramuscular
D. Submuscular

94. The name and address of the person receiving a letter is listed on the
A. Dateline
B. Letterhead
C. Attention Line
D. Inside Address

95. Acquiring funds owed to the office
A. Credit
B. Collection
C. Accounts receivable
D. Bankruptcy

96. An example of a close ended question is
A. "When was your last check-up?"
B. "How often do you take your medication?"
C. "Have you been prescribed antifungal medication?"
D. "Where was your last injection site?"

97. A spouse or child may be considered a
A. Dependent
B. Liability
C. Organization
D. Deductible

98. Depolarization of the right atrium and left atrium in an EKG is represented by
A. PR Interval
B. QRS Complex
C. P Wave
D. ST Segment

99. Catheters are responsible for
A. Draining bile from the gallbladder
B. Bringing food into the stomach
C. Draining urine from the urinary bladder
D. Draining pus from an abscess

100. The largest artery in the body
A. Aorta
B. Brachial
C. External iliac
D. Femoral

101. Bradycardia is a form of
A. Aneurysm
B. Heart murmur
C. Infarction
D. Arrythmia

102. Refraction of light through a liquid is measured by a
A. Refractometer
B. Urinometer
C. Otoscope
D. Ophthalmoscope

103. Injection administered into the dermis
A. Subcutaneous
B. Intradermal
C. Intramuscular
D. Subdermal

104. No punctuation used after Attention, Salutation, and Complimentary Closing is known as
A. Mixed Punctuation
B. Open Punctuation
C. Random Punctuation
D. Closed Punctuation

105. Being legally responsible for every aspect of a medical practice is known as
A. Consent
B. Confidentiality
C. Liability
D. Malpractice

106. Instrument used to pull, grasp, or handle tissues or equipment
A. Scissors
B. Retractor
C. Scalpel
D. Forceps

107. A centrifuge is responsible for
A. Draining the urinary bladder
B. Separating solids from liquids
C. Delivering medication in vapor form
D. Measuring blood pressure

108. A puncture produces
A. Scraping of skin
B. Jagged edges
C. A hole
D. A clean cut

109. Temperature reading taken under the tongue
A. Sublingual
B. Axillary
C. Rectal
D. Aural

110. The carotid pulse, popliteal pulse, and dorsalis pedis pulse all help to measure the following vital sign
A. Blood pressure
B. Heart rate
C. Respiration
D. Temperature

111. A business size envelope is which number
A. 10
B. 12
C. 6
D. 8

112. An error in diagnosis or treatment
A. Liability
B. Malpractice
C. Code of Ethics
D. Scope of Practice

113. All of the following are functions of the digestive system except
A. Elimination of feces
B. Absorption of nutrients
C. Break-down of food
D. Elimination of urine

114. A nephrologist would be the type of specialist referred to in all of the following conditions except
A. Lupus
B. Pitting edema
C. Pyelonephritis
D. Uremia

115. M Codes are used to
A. Identify tumors and growths
B. Describe diseases other than disease or injury
C. Classify causes of injury
D. Document up to four different conditions

116. Patient billing statements are mailed
A. Once a month
B. Twice a month
C. Once a year
D. Once every six months

117. The Complimentary Closing is placed how many lines below the body
A. One Line
B. Two Lines
C. Three Lines
D. Four Lines

118. A subcutaneous injection should enter the subcutaneous layer at what angle
A. 45 degree
B. 90 degree
C. 10 degree
D. 35 degree

119. A spirometer measures
A. Volume of urine
B. Refraction of light through a liquid
C. Volume of air intake and output
D. Amount of acidity in a substance

120. Retractors are instruments used to
A. Perform incisions
B. Grasp, pull, or handle tissue or equipment
C. Cut bandages or sutures
D. Hold tissues open

121. The right lung contains how many lobes
A. Three
B. Two
C. Four
D. One

122. A nebulizer is used to
A. Prevent introduction of microorganisms
B. Deliver medication in vapor form
C. Drain urine from the bladder
D. Separate solids from liquids

123. Medication used to prevent the formation of blood clots
A. Anticoagulant
B. Antihistamine
C. Antipyretic
D. Analgesic

124. Which of the following is not a common injection site for an intramuscular injection
A. Deltoid
B. Abdomen
C. Ventrogluteal
D. Vastus lateralis

125. Which of the following is not one of the seven nutrients
A. Amino acids
B. Protein
C. Carbohydrates
D. Fiber

126. A type of business stationary that lists name, address, and phone number at the top of the paper
A. Envelope
B. Dateline
C. Letterhead
D. Inside Address

127. An envelope that contains clasps
A. Pre-addressed
B. Padded
C. Tan Kraft
D. Dateline

128. Group Health Benefits are offered by all of the following except
A. Employers
B. Unions
C. Associations
D. Government

129. In a blood pressure reading, the higher number represents
A. Heart rate
B. Diastolic pressure
C. Arterial contraction
D. Systolic pressure

130. The definition of anatomy is
A. Study of the structure of the body
B. Study of the function of the body
C. Study of disease
D. Study of movement

131. Alpha cells in the pancreas produce
A. Glycogen
B. Insulin
C. Glucagon
D. Bile

132. Arteries carry blood in which direction
A. Between the heart chambers
B. Towards the heart
C. Away from the heart
D. Between the heart valves

133. Signs of inflammation include
A. Heat, pain, redness, coldness
B. Pain, edema, swelling, redness
C. Swelling, heat, redness, pain
D. Redness, pain, heat, dehydration

134. The most common form of hemocytometer is
A. Nebulizer
B. Newcastle
C. Neopathic
D. Neubauer

135. Most cells in the body are surrounded by
A. Cell membrane
B. Cytoplasm
C. Nucleus
D. Ribosome

136. Main type of cell that creates nervous tissue
A. Axon
B. Neuron
C. Dendrite
D. Astrocyte

137. Which of the following is not one of the four types of tissue
A. Nervous
B. Connective
C. Epithelial
D. Skeletal

138. Ringworm is a form of
A. Fungus
B. Bacteria
C. Virus
D. Parasite

139. Paralysis of the arms and legs is a condition known as
A. Paraplegia
B. Quadriplegia
C. Hemiplegia
D. Semiplegia

140. The anterior thigh is a common injection site for which type of injection
A. Intramuscular
B. Subcutaneous
C. Intradermal
D. Submuscular

141. Which of the following is used to send a letter to a specific person in a company
A. Subject Line
B. Attention Line
C. Inside Address
D. Complimentary Closing

142. When all the lines of a business letter are flushed left, it is called
A. Full Block Style
B. Modified Block Style
C. Simplified Block Style
D. Mixed Block Style

143. A scalpel is used to
A. Perform incisions
B. Close wounds
C. Pull, grasp, or handle equipment
D. Hold layers of tissue open

144. The fight or flight response is also known as
A. Sympathetic
B. Parasympathetic
C. Autonomic
D. Peripheral

145. All of the following are contagious conditions except
A. Mononucleosis
B. Cellulitis
C. Psoriasis
D. Osteomyelitis

146. Blockage of a pore may result in the development of
A. Melanoma
B. Wart
C. Lupus
D. Acne

147. Deoxygenated blood enters the heart into which chamber
A. Right ventricle
B. Right atrium
C. Left atrium
D. Left ventricle

148. The diaphragm separates which body cavities from each other
A. Abdominal and pelvic
B. Thoracic and abdominal
C. Pelvic and thoracic
D. Dorsal and ventral

149. The name is placed on which line of the address format
A. Second
B. First
C. Third
D. Fourth

150. Which of the following determines fee schedules for all health care services
A. Chapter 13 Bankruptcy
B. National Conversion Factor
C. Omnibus Budget Reconciliation Act
D. Geographical Practice Cost Index

151. Debt borrowed to be paid at a later date
A. Collection
B. Credit
C. Bankruptcy
D. Accounts Receivable

152. Sutures are used to
A. Hold tissues open
B. Prevent introduction of microorganisms
C. Cut bandages
D. Close wounds

153. An autoclave sterilizes instruments by utilizing
A. Steam
B. Bleach
C. Gravity
D. Rubbing alcohol

154. Scraped skin is produced by
A. An abrasion
B. A laceration
C. A puncture
D. An incision

155. The bones of the wrist are also called
A. Carpals
B. Tarsals
C. Metacarpals
D. Phalanges

156. Insulin is produced by which organ
A. Pancreas
B. Liver
C. Gallbladder
D. Stomach

157. Dilation of blood vessels during the inflammatory stage is controlled by
A. Histamines
B. Leukocytes
C. Neutrophils
D. Fibrosis

158. Body temperature below 90 degrees results in
A. Hypothermia
B. Heat stroke
C. Heat cramps
D. Frostbite

159. Blood in the right ventricle is
A. Oxygenated
B. Deoxygenated
C. Clotted
D. Going backwards

160. The right and left sides of the heart are separated by the
A. Pulmonary veins
B. Tricuspid valve
C. Bicuspid valve
D. Septum

161. Instrument designed to open the nasal passages for further examination
A. Ophthalmoscope
B. Nasal speculum
C. Laryngoscope
D. Autoclave

162. Instrument used to listen to sounds throughout the body
A. Electrocardiogram
B. Laryngoscope
C. Stethoscope
D. Otoscope

163. Blood in the urine, usually a result of renal failure
A. Hyperemia
B. Pyelonephritis
C. Cystitis
D. Uremia

164. Amoxycillin and methicillin are forms of
A. Macrolides
B. Penicillin
C. Cephalosporins
D. Tetracyclines

165. Acute viral infection affecting the respiratory tract
A. Influenza
B. Pneumonia
C. Pneumothorax
D. Bronchitis

166. Instrument used to test the loss of hearing
A. Stethoscope
B. Audioscope
C. Laryngoscope
D. Otoscope

167. Collection is
A. Acquiring funds owed to the office
B. Liquidation of assets
C. Debt borrowed to be paid at a later date
D. Money owed to the office

168. HIPAA was enacted in
A. 1992
B. 1986
C. 1964
D. 1996

169. The large intestine converts chyme into
A. Bolus
B. Feces
C. Water
D. Bile

170. Heat creation is produced by which type of muscle tissue
A. Smooth
B. Cardiac
C. Skeletal
D. Adipose

171. The city, state, and zip code is placed on which line in address format
A. First
B. Sixth
C. Second
D. Fourth

172. When the Dateline, Complimentary Closing, and Signature Block are centered on the page, it is called
A. Mixed Punctuation
B. Simplified Block Style
C. Full Block Style
D. Modified Block Style

173. A 90 degree angle is used when administering which injection
A. Intradermal
B. Intramuscular
C. Subcutaneous
D. Submuscular

174. Pacemakers are commonly implanted in patients who suffer from
A. Arrythmia
B. Emphysema
C. Angina pectoris
D. Heart murmur

175. Mammary glands produce what substance
A. Oil
B. Sweat
C. Milk
D. Testosterone

176. An injury to a ligament
A. Sprain
B. Strain
C. Fracture
D. Dislocation

177. Vein found in the region of the armpit
A. Inguinal vein
B. Brachial vein
C. Femoral vein
D. Axillary vein

178. The pulmonary veins carry blood from the lungs to
A. The aorta
B. The body
C. The vena cava
D. The heart

179. The body of a letter is placed how many lines below the subject
A. Two lines
B. Three lines
C. Five lines
D. One line

180. Liquidation of assets to repay debts
A. Bankruptcy
B. Collection
C. Accounts receivable
D. Credit

181. Guiding moral principles
A. Code of ethics
B. Scope of practice
C. Liability
D. Negligence

182. A medical practice owned by two or more people
A. Sole Proprietorship
B. Professional Corporation
C. Partnership
D. Group Practice

183. Certain leukocytes perform phagocytosis, which is when cells perform what action
A. Eat substances
B. Absorb nutrients
C. Move from an area of high concentration to an area of low concentration
D. Transportation of oxygen and carbon dioxide

184. Cancer of connective tissue is known as
A. Sarcoma
B. Melanoma
C. Carcinoma
D. Lymphoma

185. The formation of scar tissue
A. Hypoplasia
B. Hyperplasia
C. Fibrosis
D. Inflammatory response

186. Inflammation of a joint
A. Osteoporosis
B. Arthritis
C. Dislocation
D. Subluxation

187. Scissors are used to
A. Perform incisions
B. Hold layers of tissue open
C. Close wounds
D. Cut tissue or bandages

188. The extend of a burn by total body area involved is determined by
A. First degree
B. The Rule of 9's
C. Quadrants
D. Contacting EMS

189. Expiration is also known as
A. Tidal volume
B. Blood pressure
C. Exhaling
D. Inhaling

190. The skin produces the following type of vitamin
A. Vitamin K
B. Vitamin A
C. Vitamin D
D. Vitamin B12

191. Storage of urine is found in the
A. Kidneys
B. Gallbladder
C. Bladder
D. Urethra

192. An eletroencephalogram measures
A. Muscle contractions
B. Heart rhythm
C. Blood pressure
D. Brain wave activity

193. A lack of hemoglobin in erythrocytes may result in
A. Decreased immune response
B. Raynaud's syndrome
C. Myocardial infarction
D. Anemia

194. Of the following, which condition is contagious
A. Ankylosing spondylitis
B. Osteoporosis
C. Trigeminal neuralgia
D. Mononucleosis

195. A wart is caused by
A. Parasite
B. Bacteria
C. Fungus
D. Virus

196. The inferior chambers of the heart are known as
A. Atria
B. Ventricles
C. Vena Cava
D. Aorta

197. Instrument used to test reflexes
A. Otoscope
B. Stethoscope
C. Percussion hammer
D. Forceps

198. An open-ended question is
A. Used when asking for feedback from a patient
B. Used to ask a patient if they have a heart condition
C. Used when only looking for a yes or no response
D. Used when a patient has allergies

199. The most abundant form of connective tissue found in the body
A. Fascia
B. Bone
C. Cartilage
D. Blood

200. The trachea is also known as
A. Windpipe
B. Lung
C. Throat
D. Voice box

1. D	41. B	81. C	121. A	161. B
2. A	42. D	82. B	122. B	162. C
3. C	43. A	83. C	123. A	163. D
4. B	44. D	84. C	124. B	164. B
5. C	45. B	85. D	125. A	165. A
6. A	46. D	86. A	126. C	166. B
7. C	47. A	87. C	127. C	167. A
8. C	48. A	88. D	128. D	168. D
9. A	49. A	89. A	129. D	169. B
10. D	50. C	90. C	130. A	170. C
11. A	51. C	91. A	131. C	171. D
12. A	52. C	92. D	132. C	172. D
13. B	53. A	93. C	133. C	173. B
14. C	54. C	94. D	134. D	174. A
15. B	55. B	95. B	135. A	175. C
16. D	56. A	96. C	136. B	176. A
17. B	57. C	97. A	137. D	177. D
18. C	58. C	98. C	138. A	178. D
19. C	59. A	99. C	139. B	179. A
20. A	60. D	100. A	140. B	180. A
21. A	61. B	101. D	141. B	181. A
22. D	62. C	102. A	142. A	182. C
23. D	63. A	103. B	143. A	183. A
24. C	64. A	104. B	144. A	184. A
25. B	65. D	105. C	145. C	185. C
26. A	66. C	106. D	146. D	186. B
27. A	67. A	107. B	147. B	187. D
28. A	68. A	108. C	148. B	188. B
29. A	69. A	109. A	149. B	189. C
30. B	70. D	110. B	150. B	190. C
31. A	71. C	111. A	151. B	191. C
32. B	72. A	112. B	152. D	192. D
33. C	73. D	113. D	153. A	193. D
34. B	74. B	114. A	154. A	194. D
35. A	75. C	115. A	155. A	195. D
36. A	76. D	116. A	156. A	196. B
37. A	77. A	117. B	157. A	197. C
38. D	78. D	118. A	158. A	198. A
39. A	79. D	119. C	159. B	199. D
40. C	80. B	120. D	160. D	200. A

1. The second phase of inflammation is called phagocytosis, which is the responsibility of
A. Leukocytes
B. Erythrocytes
C. Thrombocytes
D. Histamines

2. In a client with herpes simplex, exposure to sunlight, stress, or hormonal changes may result in the development of
A. Impetigo
B. Decubitus ulcers
C. Cold sores
D. Acne

3. Inhalation and expiration contribute to which vital sign
A. Repiration
B. Blood pressure
C. Pulse
D. Temperature

4. The apical pulse helps to read heart rhythm and rate at what point in the body
A. Medial wrist
B. Apex of the heart
C. Proximal anterior thigh
D. Back of the knee

5. Natural pacemaker of the body, responsible for contracting the right and left ventricles
A. Phrenic nerve
B. Papillary muscles
C. SA node
D. Coronary arteries

6. The Rule of 9's is used to
A. Determine the nine regions of the body used to divide the abdomen
B. Determine the nine sections of the tongue that taste
C. Determine the extent of burns by total body area involved
D. Determine the gauge of a needle used for injections

7. E Codes are used to
A. Indentify tumors and growths
B. Document procedures
C. Circumstances other than disease or injury
D. Classify cause of injury, poisoning, or adverse reaction to drugs

8. An incision produces
A. A hole
B. Jagged edges
C. Scraped skin
D. A clean cut

9. Which type of gland has no ducts
A. Endocrine
B. Exocrine
C. Eccrine
D. Mammary

10. Follicle-stimulating hormone, produced by the pituitary gland, affects what other structure in the body
A. Ovaries
B. Testes
C. Pancreas
D. Thyroid

11. A percussion hammer is used to test
A. Reflexes
B. Blood pressure
C. Electrical activity in the heart
D. Hearing loss

12. A sublingual temperature reading is taken
A. Inside the ear
B. Inside the rectum
C. Under the tongue
D. Under the armpit

13. Melanoma is what type of tumor
A. Benign
B. Malignant
C. Idiopathic
D. Lymphatic

14. Swelling of the following gland results in a goiter
A. Pituitary
B. Thyroid
C. Thymus
D. Adrenal

15. The function of the mouth
A. Absorption
B. Mastication
C. Excretion
D. Secretion

16. Treating every person and fluid as infectious is known as
A. Emergency triage
B. Documentation
C. Contamination
D. Universal precautions

17. Thin connective tissue surrounding the brain and spinal cord, primarily responsible for providing protection
A. Pericardium
B. Serous membrane
C. Meninges
D. Peritoneal membrane

18. Insulin is secreted by the following
A. Alpha cells
B. Beta cells
C. Delta cells
D. Theta cells

19. A collection agency is used to
A. Liquidate assets
B. Borrow debt
C. Acquire assets
D. Collect outstanding debts

20. A bacterial infection that enters the blood stream results in
A. Septicemia
B. Anemia
C. Gout
D. Leukemia

21. Vomiting is also known as
A. Defecation
B. Reflux
C. Emesis
D. GERD

22. Melatonin levels in the body fluctuate in response to the
A. Circadian rhythm
B. Heart rhythm
C. Circulatory system
D. Lymphatic system

23. Alveoli are located at the ends of
A. Pulmonary veins
B. Bronchial tubes
C. Bronchioles
D. Trachea

24. A colon after the Attention and Salutation is used in which type of punctuation
A. Open Punctuation
B. Random Punctuation
C. Closed Punctuation
D. Mixed Punctuation

25. The most common form of Vitamin A is
A. Calcium
B. Beta-carotene
C. Iron
D. Sodium

26. Which of the following part of blood is responsible for clotting of the blood in response to physical trauma
A. White blood cells
B. Red blood cells
C. Platelets
D. Plasma

27. An intradermal injection is administered into the
A. Subcutaneous layer
B. Epidermis
C. Dermis
D. Muscle

28. Which of the following is a visualization of the firing of an SA node
A. PR Interval
B. T Wave
C. P Wave
D. QRS Complex

29. A sphygmomanometer measures
A. Blood pressure
B. Heart rate
C. Volume of intake and output of air
D. Gravity of urine

30. The small intestine
A. Breaks down food into usable parts for absorption
B. Absorbs water from feces and eliminates waste
C. Absorbs nutrients from chyme into the blood
D. Transports food from the mouth to the stomach

31. Device used to separate solids from liquids
A. Nebulizer
B. Centrifuge
C. Sphygmomanometer
D. Spirometer

32. Well-defined borders of infection is typical of which condition
A. Contusion
B. Osteomyelitis
C. Thrush
D. Cellulitis

33. Medication given to people who suffer from asthma to relax smooth muscle in the respiratory system
A. Bronchodilators
B. Expectorants
C. Decongestants
D. Statins

34. Which of the following is used to inform the recipient of the subject of a letter
A. Signature Block
B. Attention Line
C. Salutation
D. Subject Line

35. Which of the following is not a common injection site for a subcutaneous injection
A. Scapula
B. Abdomen
C. Posterior and lateral arm
D. Anterior thigh

36. Vitamin D allows the body to absorb
A. Sodium
B. Beta-carotene
C. Potassium
D. Calcium

37. Endocarditis
A. Inflammation of the muscle of the heart
B. Inflammation of the inner linings of the heart
C. Inflammation of the connective tissue surrounding the heart
D. Inflammation of the coronary arteries

38. A contusion is also known as
A. Bruise
B. Wart
C. Fracture
D. Hives

39. The kidneys
A. Reabsorbs urea into the blood stream and removes
water
B. Eliminates waste from the bladder
C. Filter waste from the blood and reabsorb substances into the body
D. Produces norepinephrine to assist with the sympathetic nervous response

40. A Tan Kraft envelope contains
A. Clasps
B. Padding
C. Pre-addressed envelope
D. Letterhead

41. Which of the following is considered one of the four types of tissue in the body
A. Nervous
B. Smooth
C. Skeletal
D. Hair

42. A 10 to 15 degree angle is used in which injection
A. Intramuscular
B. Subcutaneous
C. Intradermal
D. Submuscular

43. Pseudoepinephrine is a substance found in the following medications
A. Antihistamines
B. Expectorants
C. Bronchodilators
D. Decongestants

44. Necrosis of myocardium due to blockages in the coronary arteries leads to
A. Aneurysm
B. Heart murmur
C. Myocardial infarction
D. Arrythmia

45. Urine flows from the kidneys through the ureters on its way to the
A. Urethra
B. Bladder
C. Bloodstream
D. Liver

46. The smallest type of blood vessel
A. Capillary
B. Artery
C. Vein
D. Arteriole

47. Malpractice is
A. An error in diagnosis or treatment
B. Being legally responsible for every aspect of a medical practice
C. Keeping information private and protected
D. Guiding moral principles

48. Medicare provides health insurance to
A. Low-income persons
B. Elderly
C. Dependents of active military personnel
D. Retired military personnel

49. Which of the following is not a main group of food
A. Lipids
B. Protein
C. Carbohydrates
D. Insulin

50. Vitamin A is produced and stored by the
A. Gallbladder
B. Liver
C. Spleen
D. Small intestine

51. Which of the following is used to document up to four different conditions
A. M Codes
B. ICD-9-CM
C. E Codes
D. CMS-1500

52. A collection of pus, usually localized
A. Psoriasis
B. Lesion
C. Wart
D. Abscess

53. A medical practice owned by one person
A. Partnership
B. Sole Proprietorship
C. Group Practice
D. Professional Corporation

54. Failure to perform essential actions that results in hard to a patient
A. Malpractice
B. Negligence
C. Liability
D. Consent

55. Inflammation of the kidneys
A. Hepatitis
B. Nephritis
C. Cystitis
D. Gastritis

56. Bronchodilators, expectorants, and decongestants all affect the
A. Respiratory system
B. Endocrine system
C. Nervous system
D. Cardiovascular system

57. Diarrhea may result in
A. Diverticulosis
B. Constipation
C. Ulcerative colitis
D. Dehydration

58. Type of drug that combats bacterial infection
A. Morphine
B. Antibiotics
C. Non-steroidal anti-inflammatory drugs
D. Immunizations

59. Collection is
A. Acquiring funds owed to the office
B. Liquidation of assets
C. Debt borrowed to be paid at a later date
D. Money owed to the office

60. The Attention Line is used to
A. Send a letter to a specific person in a company
B. Note the month, day, and year a letter is sent
C. Note the address, name, and phone number of a business
D. Inform the reader what the subject of a letter is

61. Allergic reactions in the body may be controlled with use of
A. Vasodilators
B. Statins
C. Antihistamines
D. Beta-blockers

62. The dateline contains which information
A. Month, day, and year
B. Name, address, and phone number
C. Name and address of person receiving the letter
D. Courtesy title

63. A subcutaneous injection enters into the
A. Subcutaneous layer
B. Dermis
C. Epidermis
D. Muscle

64. The four types of tissue found in the body are
A. Muscular, smooth, skeletal, cardiac
B. Epithelial, connective, nervous, muscular
C. Epithelial, skeletal, connective, nervous
D. Connective, epithelial, nervous, smooth

65. Ureters transport what substance
A. Blood
B. Urine
C. Lymph
D. Feces

66. The aorta carries blood to the liver via the
A. Carotid artery
B. Renal artery
C. Hepatic artery
D. Pulmonary artery

67. The diameter of a needle is known as
A. Gauge
B. Stopper
C. Plunger
D. Point

68. Lungs and kidneys are both examples of
A. Paired organs
B. Digestive organs
C. Respiratory organs
D. Urinary organs

69. Small glass container which is broken at the neck to access medication
A. Vial
B. Ampule
C. Gauge
D. Needle

70. Pressure felt as blood passes through an artery
A. Diastolic
B. Systolic
C. Venous
D. Cardiac

71. During the fight or flight response, what body function shuts down
A. Movement
B. Circulation
C. Respiration
D. Digestion

72. Keeping patient information private and protected
A. Liability
B. Confidentiality
C. Malpractice
D. Informed Consent

73. Medicaid provides health care to
A. Elderly
B. Dependents of active military personnel
C. Low-income persons
D. Active military personnel

74. A T Wave is
A. Depolarization of the right ventricle and left ventricle
B. Repolarization of the right ventricle and left ventricle
C. Depolarization of the right atrium and left atrium
D. Time taken for a nerve impulse to travel from an SA node through atria into ventricles

75. Pain relievers are also known as
A. Antibiotics
B. Broncho-dilators
C. Diuretics
D. Analgesics

76. Embolism
A. Bulge in an artery wall, usually caused by a weakened artery due to a condition such as hypertension
B. Inflammation of a vein due to trauma, resulting in blood clot formation
C. Blood clot in the blood stream becoming lodged in the heart, lungs, or brain, resulting in death of tissue
D. Ischemia in the myocardium due to a blockage in the coronary arteries, resulting in myocardial infarction

77. An artifact in an EKG reading is
A. An abnormality of non-cardiac origin
B. An abnormality caused by a pacemaker
C. A medical instrument that sends electrical impulses through the heart
D. A flatline

78. A refractometer measures
A. Volume of air intake and output
B. Gravity of urine
C. Refraction of light through a liquid
D. Blood pressure

79. Aged red blood cells are destroyed in the following organ
A. Liver
B. Stomach
C. Pancreas
D. Spleen

80. Pressure felt in the walls of arteries when blood is not passing through
A. Systolic
B. Diastolic
C. Venous
D. Cardiac

81. The most common form of cancer is found in the
A. Breast
B. Lungs
C. Pancreas
D. Skin

82. Which of the following adjusts physician fees
A. Omnibus Budget Reconciliation Act
B. National Conversion Factor
C. Geographical Practice Cost Index
D. Chapter 7 Brankruptcy

83. The Signature Block should be placed how many lines below the Complimentary Closing
A. Four Lines
B. Two Lines
C. Three Lines
D. Five Lines

84. Sublingual, axillary, rectal, and aural are all regions used to measure
A. Temperature
B. Blood pressure
C. Pulse
D. Respiration

85. The trachea is also known as
A. Windpipe
B. Lung
C. Throat
D. Voice box

86. The left atrium receives blood from the
A. Pulmonary arteries
B. Pulmonary veins
C. Superior vena cava
D. Inferior vena cava

87. Atrial fibrillation is a form of
A. Heart murmur
B. Arrythmia
C. Infarction
D. Aneurysm

88. Ibuprofen and acetaminophen are examples of
A. Antihistamines
B. Anti-inflammatory
C. Diuretics
D. Antipyretics

89. Lack of calcium entering into the bone can lead to
A. Scoliosis
B. Osteomyelitis
C. Dowager's hump
D. Osteoporosis

90. Contraction of the ventricles causes
A. Systole
B. Diastole
C. Dilation
D. Embolism

91. Inspiration is also known as
A. Inhaling
B. Exhaling
C. Tidal volume
D. Blood pressure

92. Hormone responsible for increasing heart rate and moving blood from digestive organs into the muscles
A. Aldosterone
B. Oxytocin
C. Growth hormone
D. Norepinephrine

93. Normal cells growing uncontrollably results in
A. Inflammation
B. Cyst
C. Cancer
D. Edema

94. Osteomyelitis and the most serious form of meningitis are the result of
A. Fungus
B. Bacteria
C. Virus
D. Parasite

95. Personal protective equipment helps to
A. Protect against lawsuits
B. Protect against infectious agents
C. Protect against weather
D. Protect against confidentiality

96. A QRS Complex is
A. Repolarization of right ventricle and left ventricle
B. Depolarization of the right atrium and left atrium
C. Conduction of an electrical impulse from the bundle of His through the ventricles
D. Depolarization of right ventricle and left ventricle

97. The amount required to be paid by a policy-holder before insurance payment begin
A. Dependent
B. Malpractice
C. Deductible
D. Bankruptcy

98. The inferior chambers of the heart are known as
A. Atria
B. Ventricles
C. Vena Cava
D. Aorta

99. Endocrine glands secrete their substances where
A. Into the respiratory passages
B. Onto a surface
C. Into the blood
D. Into the digestive organs

100. Accounts receivable
A. Money owed to the office
B. Acquiring funds or payment owed to the office
C. Debt borrowed to be paid at a later date
D. Assets sold off and funds distributed to creditors

101. Passive listening is
A. Listening to the patient and replying to statements being made
B. Questions used when asking for feedback
C. Questions that require only a yes or no response
D. Listening to the patient without offering a reply

102. Urea, ammonia, and creatinine are filtered from the body and form
A. Urine
B. Sweat
C. Oil
D. Feces

103. Structure in the throat providing vibration of air to produce voice
A. Trachea
B. Pharynx
C. Esophagus
D. Larynx

104. Shortness of breath
A. Dyspnea
B. Apnea
C. Asthma
D. Bronchitis

105. Health insurance provided to the elderly which is sponsored by the government
A. Medicaid
B. TRICARE
C. Medicare
D. PPO

106. Which of the following is not a common injection site for an intradermal injection
A. Anterior forearm
B. Thorax
C. Scapula
D. Vastus lateralis

107. Antibodies play what role in the body's defense against pathogens
A. Destroy foreign substances
B. Engulf particles
C. Carrier cells for immunity
D. Create leukocytes

108. Function of cardiac muscle
A. Movement
B. Heat creation
C. Peristalsis
D. Transportation

109. Cholelithiasis is also known as
A. Gallstones
B. Kidney stones
C. Blood clot
D. Aneurysm

110. An antipyretic is a type of medication responsible for
A. Eliminating increased glucose
B. Decreasing inflammation
C. Destroying bacteria
D. Lowering fever

111. Infection of the skin by staphylococcus or streptococcus bacteria, forming yellowish scabs and sores around the mouth and nose
A. Psoriasis
B. Cold sore
C. Impetigo
D. Cellulitis

112. An increase of non-functioning leukocytes entering into medullary cavities may result in
A. Leukemia
B. Anemia
C. Melanoma
D. Non-Hodgkins Lymphoma

113. Certain leukocytes perform phagocytosis, which is when cells perform what action
A. Eat substances
B. Absorb nutrients
C. Move from an area of high concentration to an area of low concentration
D. Transportation of oxygen and carbon dioxide

114. The thorax is a common injection site for which type of injection
A. Intradermal
B. Intramuscular
C. Subcutaneous
D. Submuscular

115. Letter style that includes no Salutation with the Subject placed between the Address and Body
A. Mixed Punctuation
B. Simplified Style
C. Modified Block Style
D. Full Block Style

116. Which of the following are used to close wounds
A. Sutures
B. Dressings
C. Bandages
D. Retractors

117. Food moves from the small intestine into the following part of the large intestine
A. Sigmoid colon
B. Ascending colon
C. Cecum
D. Transverse colon

118. Sebum is produced by which type of gland
A. Mammary
B. Sudoriferous
C. Adrenal
D. Sebaceous

119. A catheter is
A. A tube inserted into the bladder
B. A tube inserted into the large intestine
C. A tube inserted into the esophagus
D. A tube inserted into the trachea

120. Which of the following adjusts physician fees
A. Omnibus Budget Reconciliation Act
B. National Conversion Factor
C. Geographical Practice Cost Index
D. Chapter 7 Brankruptcy

121. A client with Crohn's disease would be referred to which doctor
A. Gastroenterologist
B. Nephrologist
C. Neurologist
D. Dermatologist

122. Chronic bronchitis and emphysema are examples of
A. Chronic obstructive pulmonary disease
B. Asthma
C. Pleurisy
D. Congestive heart failure

123. Part of the brain split into two hemispheres
A. Cerebellum
B. Cerebrum
C. Brain stem
D. Diencephalon

124. The four regions of the lower limb
A. Femur, tibia, calcaneus, hallux
B. Thigh, leg, ankle, foot
C. Thigh, shin, ankle, foot
D. Leg, calf, ankle, foot

125. A PR Interval represents
A. Conduction of electrical impulse from bundle of His through ventricles
B. Depolarization of the right atrium and right ventricle
C. Depolarization of the right ventricle and left ventricle
D. Time taken for an impulse to travel from the SA node through the atria into ventricles

126. A 45 degree angle is used in which type of injection
A. Submuscular
B. Intradermal
C. Subcutaneous
D. Intramuscular

127. An ophthalmoscope is used to inspect
A. The ears
B. The eyes
C. The large intestine
D. The mouth

128. Pennate and spiral are both types of
A. Muscles
B. Nerves
C. Organs
D. Connective tissue

129. Proteins are broken down into the following via digestive enzymes
A. Glucose
B. Amino acids
C. Lipids
D. Fructose

130. Peripheral vascular disease is usually the result of what other condition
A. Atherosclerosis
B. Myocardial infarction
C. Aneurysm
D. Muscular dystrophy

131. Thinning of mucous in the respiratory passages can be aided by which type of medication
A. Bronchodilator
B. Decongestant
C. Expectorant
D. Anticoagulant

132. Needles are used to
A. Administer injections
B. Contain pathogens
C. Relieve pain
D. Store medications

133. Which of the following type of muscle tissue is found in the heart
A. Skeletal
B. Cardiac
C. Smooth
D. Pyloric

134. Bone located in the thigh
A. Tibia
B. Femur
C. Fibula
D. Talus

135. Thrombosis
A. Creation of a blood clot within a blood vessel
B. Blood clot blocking a valve in the heart
C. Weakening of an arterial wall, resulting in necrosis
D. Blockage of coronary arteries in the heart, producing an infarct

136. The first line in address format is
A. Name
B. Address
C. City and State
D. Zip code

137. Instrument used to hold layers of tissue open, allowing access to underlying tissue
A. Forceps
B. Scalpel
C. Retractor
D. Scissors

138. The emergency triage is
A. Classifying injuries by treatment urgency, treatment location, and severity
B. Noting all patient emergencies
C. Treating any fluid as contaminated
D. Wearing gloves and protective equipment

139. An intramuscular injection enters into the muscle at what angle
A. 45 degree
B. 15 degree
C. 90 degree
D. 10 degree

140. Bacterial infection affecting the kidneys as a result of a urinary tract infection
A. Necrotising fasciitis
B. Cystitis
C. Pancreatitis
D. Pyelonephritis

141. Rupture of a cerebral aneurysm results in
A. Thrombosis
B. Stroke
C. Embolism
D. Myocardial infarction

142. A container sealed by a rubber stopper at the top is known as
A. Ampule
B. Insulin
C. Needle
D. Vial

143. Instrument used to deliver medication in vapor form
A. Bronchodilator
B. Beta-Blocker
C. Nebulizer
D. Electrocardiograph

144. Blood pressure is one of the primary means used to measure
A. Repiration
B. Temperature
C. Heart rhythm
D. Vital signs

145. Epithelial tissue is found in all of the following parts of the body except
A. Skin
B. Lungs
C. Heart
D. Intestines

146. The organization of a structure in the body
A. Organ → Tissue → Cell
B. Cell → Tissue → Organ
C. Cell → Organ → Tissue
D. Tissue → Cell → Organ

147. Pain in the chest and left arm resulting from myocardial ischemia
A. Angina pectoris
B. Atherosclerosis
C. Arteriosclerosis
D. Phlebitis

148. Which of the following is not a normal site to measure heart rate
A. Radial pulse
B. Brachial pulse
C. Axillary pulse
D. Femoral pulse

149. A stethoscope is used to
A. Inspect inner portions of the eye
B. Inspect the tympanic membrane
C. Open the nasal passages
D. Listen to sounds throughout the body

150. Temperature is used to measure
A. Lung intake
B. Heart rate
C. Pressure in arteries
D. Body heat

151. Epinephrine and norepinephrine are produced by the
A. Thalamus
B. Pineal gland
C. Pituitary gland
D. Adrenal glands

152. Of the following, which condition is contagious
A. Influenza
B. Osteoarthritis
C. Raynaud's disease
D. Sebaceous cyst

153. An otoscope allows visual inspection of
A. Ears
B. Eyes
C. Nose
D. Mouth

154. A margin is
A. An area around the edges of a form
B. Lists the name, address, and phone number at the top of the paper
C. Contains the month, day, and year
D. Name and address of the person receiving the letter

155. The regularity of a heart beat is known as
A. Heart rate
B. Systolic pressure
C. Heart rhythm
D. Diastolic pressure

156. Temperature, blood pressure, pulse, and respiration contribute to the reading of
A. Heart rhythm
B. Vital signs
C. Systolic pressure
D. Diastolic pressure

157. The pulmonary arteries carry
A. Deoxygenated blood
B. Oxygenated blood
C. Clotted blood
D. No blood

158. Upon stimulation of the sympathetic nervous response, the following reaction takes place in the heart
A. No change
B. Decreased heart rate
C. Increased heart rate
D. Cardiac arrest

159. Forceps are used to
A. Handle, pull, or grasp tissues or equipment
B. Hold layers of tissue open
C. Close tissues
D. Sterilization of equipment

160. Small knife used to perform incisions
A. Forceps
B. Scalpel
C. Retractor
D. Scissors

161. The large intestine
A. Digests and breaks down food
B. Absorbs nutrients from chyme
C. Eliminates waste and absorbs water from fecal matter
D. Reabsorbs electrolytes into the blood stream

162. The sublingual salivary glands are located beneath the
A. Ears
B. Tongue
C. Nose
D. Mandible

163. Medical device used to view objects not visible to the naked eye
A. Centrifuge
B. Nebulizer
C. Microscope
D. Otoscope

164. Trauma to a vein may result in
A. Varicose veins
B. Phlebitis
C. Arteriosclerosis
D. Anemia

165. Laryngitis may result in
A. Decreased tidal volume
B. Loss of voice
C. Difficulty swallowing
D. Increase thyroid production

166. Shaking of a part of the body that is involuntary
A. Tourette's syndrome
B. Paralysis
C. Tremor
D. Trigeminal neuralgia

167. Secretion is performed by which structures in the body
A. Muscles
B. Bones
C. Glands
D. Nerves

168. An autoclave is a medical device used to
A. Separate solids from liquids
B. Pull, grasp, or handle tissue or equipment
C. Hold layers of tissue open
D. Sterilize instruments

169. The tricuspid valve is located between which two structures
A. Left ventricle and aorta
B. Left atrium and left ventricle
C. Stomach and esophagus
D. Right atrium and right ventricle

170. Bile is produced by the
A. Gallbladder
B. Liver
C. Stomach
D. Pancreas

171. Instrument used to cut tissue, bandages, or sutures
A. Scalpel
B. Forceps
C. Staples
D. Scissors

172. Low-density lipoprotein levels in the body can be reduced with the use of
A. Antihistamines
B. Beta-blockers
C. Statins
D. Expectorants

173. Heart murmur
A. Necrosis of myocardium due to blockages in coronary arteries
B. Irregular heart rhythm due to random electrical impulses stimulating myocardium of ventricles
C. Hole in the ventricular septum, resulting in blood passing freely between ventricles
D. Blood flow moving backwards in the heart due to valve incompetence

174. Location of the sinoatrial node
A. Left ventricle
B. Right ventricle
C. Left atrium
D. Right atrium

175. Type of microscope used to count blood cells and thrombocytes
A. Hemocytometer
B. Centrifuge
C. Sphygmomanometer
D. Nebulizer

176. Which of the following contributes to the measurement of vital signs
A. Temperature
B. Injections
C. Skin rigidity
D. Pupil dilation

177. The ulnar pulse helps to read heart rhythm and rate at what point in the body
A. Lateral wrist
B. Back of the knee
C. Dorsal surface of the foot
D. Medial wrist

178. A doctor that specializes in the feet is known as a
A. Podiatrist
B. Oncologist
C. Radiologist
D. Rheumatologist

179. Pulmonary edema
A. Excessive fluid in the lungs
B. Blood clot in the lungs
C. Reduction of circulation to the lungs
D. Degeneration of alveoli in the lungs

180. Mesentery is part of which serous membrane
A. Pleural
B. Pericardium
C. Peritoneal
D. Meninges

181. Ureters connect which two structures together
A. Liver and gallbladder
B. Bladder and urethra
C. Small intestine and pancreas
D. Kidneys and bladder

182. A vital sign reading of 120/80 mmHg measures
A. Pulse
B. Respiration
C. Temperature
D. Blood pressure

183. All of the following are locations utilized to measure temperature except
A. Axilla
B. Rectum
C. Oral cavity
D. Olecranon

184. Substance found in erythrocytes which attaches to oxygen and carbon dioxide, allowing transport of these molecules to parts of the body
A. Platelets
B. Leukocyte
C. Anemia
D. Hemoglobin

185. Heart activity is detected via an
A. Ophthalmoscope
B. Electroencephalogram
C. Audiometer
D. Electrocardiogram

186. Inflammation of the pleural membrane, resulting in chest pain
A. Bronchitis
B. Pneumonia
C. Pleurisy
D. Asthma

187. A gastrologist is a doctor that specializes in
A. Skin
B. Heart
C. Stomach
D. Connective tissue

188. Vital sign measuring the body's heat
A. Pulse
B. Temperature
C. Blood pressure
D. Respiration

189. Study of the function of the human body
A. Anatomy
B. Physiology
C. Pathology
D. Etiology

190. The urinary bladder is found in which body cavity
A. Cranial
B. Abdominal
C. Thoracic
D. Pelvic

191. Heart beats per minute is known as
A. Heart rate
B. Diastolic pressure
C. Systolic pressure
D. Heart rhythm

192. Osteoarthritis is also known as
A. De Qurevain's disease
B. Rheumatoid arthritis
C. Wear and tear arthritis
D. Carpal tunnel syndrome

193. Neurotransmitter involved in the trembling movements involved with Parkison's disease
A. Dopamine
B. Epinephrine
C. Norepinephrine
D. Melatonin

194. Blockage of the ureters by a kidney stone results in
A. Pyelonephritis
B. Cystitis
C. Uremia
D. Hydronephritis

195. Vital sign which measures systolic and diastolic pressure
A. Temperature
B. Respiration
C. Blood pressure
D. Pulse

196. The cerebellum is formed by which type of tissue
A. Connective
B. Nervous
C. Epithelial
D. Muscular

197. All of the following are contagious conditions except
A. Mononucleosis
B. Herpes simplex
C. Arrythmia
D. Osteomyelitis

198. The final stage of an HIV infection is known as
A. AIDS
B. PPALM
C. ARC
D. HBV

199. The heart contains how many chambers
A. Four
B. Two
C. Three
D. Five

200. Glucagon is a digestive enzyme produced in the pancreas by
A. Alpha cells
B. Beta cells
C. Lymphatic tissue
D. Erythrocytes

1. A	41. A	81. D	121. A	161. C
2. C	42. C	82. C	122. A	162. B
3. A	43. D	83. A	123. B	163. C
4. B	44. C	84. A	124. B	164. B
5. C	45. B	85. A	125. D	165. B
6. D	46. A	86. B	126. C	166. C
7. D	47. A	87. B	127. B	167. C
8. A	48. B	88. D	128. A	168. D
9. A	49. D	89. D	129. B	169. D
10. A	50. B	90. A	130. A	170. B
11. A	51. D	91. A	131. C	171. D
12. C	52. D	92. D	132. A	172. C
13. B	53. B	93. C	133. B	173. D
14. B	54. B	94. B	134. B	174. D
15. B	55. B	95. B	135. A	175. A
16. D	56. A	96. C	136. A	176. A
17. C	57. D	97. C	137. C	177. D
18. B	58. B	98. B	138. A	178. A
19. D	59. A	99. C	139. C	179. A
20. A	60. A	100. A	140. D	180. C
21. C	61. C	101. D	141. B	181. D
22. A	62. A	102. A	142. D	182. D
23. C	63. A	103. D	143. C	183. D
24. D	64. B	104. A	144. D	184. D
25. B	65. B	105. C	145. C	185. D
26. C	66. C	106. D	146. B	186. C
27. C	67. A	107. A	147. A	187. C
28. C	68. A	108. D	148. C	188. B
29. A	69. B	109. A	149. D	189. B
30. C	70. B	110. D	150. D	190. D
31. B	71. D	111. C	151. D	191. A
32. D	72. B	112. A	152. A	192. C
33. A	73. C	113. A	153. A	193. A
34. D	74. B	114. A	154. A	194. D
35. A	75. D	115. B	155. C	195. C
36. D	76. C	116. A	156. B	196. B
37. B	77. A	117. C	157. A	197. C
38. A	78. C	118. D	158. C	198. A
39. C	79. D	119. A	159. A	199. A
40. A	80. B	120. C	160. B	200. A

References

All of the following were used in the creation of this study guide:

The Four Hour Chef – Timothy Ferriss, 2013
Anatomica: The Complete Home Medical Reference – Ken Ashwell, 2010
Pharmacology for Massage Therapy – Jean Wible, 2004
Pearson's Comprehensive Medical Assisting, Second Edition –
Nina Beaman, MS, RNC, CMA, 2010
Medical Assisting Review: Passing the CMA, RMA, and CCMA Exams –
Jahangir Moini, 2011
Mosby's Pathology for Massage Therapy – Susan Salvo, Sandra Anderson,
2004
http://www.nlm.nih.gov/medlineplus/ency/article/002400.htm
http://www.nlm.nih.gov/medlineplus/ency/article/002407.htm
http://www.nlm.nih.gov/medlineplus/ency/article/002405.htm
http://www.nlm.nih.gov/medlineplus/ency/article/002406.htm
http://www.nlm.nih.gov/medlineplus/ency/article/002404.htm
http://www.nlm.nih.gov/medlineplus/ency/article/002402.htm
http://www.nlm.nih.gov/medlineplus/ency/article/002403.htm
http://www.nlm.nih.gov/medlineplus/potassium.html
http://www.nlm.nih.gov/medlineplus/calcium.html
http://www.nlm.nih.gov/medlineplus/iron.html
http://www.nlm.nih.gov/medlineplus/ency/article/002415.htm
http://www.nlm.nih.gov/medlineplus/ency/article/002423.htm

A special thank you to Barbara Aberle for all the help!

48699175R10104

Made in the USA
Charleston, SC
07 November 2015